W0035893

04
A U I D series

AUID series presents texts extracted from the final doctoral dissertations of the Doctoral Program in Architectural Urban Interior Design (AUID) at Politecnico di Milano, Department of Architecture and Urban Studies.

Editor
Francesca Zanotto
Graphic Design
Francesco Trovato

AUID Head
Alessandro Rocca

AUID Scientific Board
Guya Bertelli, Marco Biraghi, Marco Borsotti, Marco Bovati, Margitta Buchert, Pier Federico Caliari, Simona Chiodo, Luigi Cocchiarella, Emilia Corradi, Valentina Dessì, Andrea Di Franco, Immacolata C. Forino, Roberto Gigliotti, Matthias Graf von Ballestrem, Andrea Gritti, Laura Montedoro, Carles Muro, Marco Navarra, Filippo Orsini, Orsina Simona Pierini, Gennaro Postiglione, Alessandro Rocca, Alessandro Rogora, Pierluigi Salvadeo, Luigi Spinelli, Ilaria Valente

POLITECNICO
MILANO 1863

DIPARTIMENTO DI ARCHITETTURA
E STUDI URBANI
DEPARTMENT OF ARCHITECTURE
AND URBAN STUDIES

AUID series

These agile booklets document the research carried out within our doctoral program. We decided not to publish the entire doctoral works, which are extensive and articulated, but to, instead, select and extract, from those scientific concentrates of sophisticated knowledge, the most comprehensible studies that are obviously associated with themes of the current debate on architectural design. These texts have, therefore, been forcibly stripped of their premises, of the state of the art and apparatus overview. They have, at times, even been disconnected from the broader rationale they belonged to. Hence, it is an arbitrary and, sometimes, unjust process, if we consider the scientific coherence of the original constructs. However, dear reader, we assure you that it was done with the best of intentions, an effort aimed at building a small, solid and well-designed bridge between the elite world of academic research and the fluid, open and permeable to discussion, updates of the critical evolution of contemporary architectural design.

Alessandro Rocca

The author thanks all the supervisors for their guidance in carrying on this research during his Ph.D. studies. A special mention goes to Prof. Luca Maria Francesco Fabris for his constant support and priceless advice in this adventure.

–

This book presents an elaboration of selected chapters from author's doctoral thesis: *Design Challenges in Zhangyang Village, Fujian Province. Rural Revitalisation in the Chinese New Era*, supervised by professors Ilaria Valente and Wenjun Ma; co-supervised by professors Luca Maria Francesco Fabris and Jianyun Huang. In 2020, the thesis was successfully defended at both the Department of Architecture and Urban Studies, Politecnico di Milano and at the School of Design, Shanghai Jiao Tong University.

ISBN 978-88-6242-545-2

First edition January 2022

© LetteraVentidue Edizioni
© Gerardo Semprebon

Reproduction of part or all of the contents in any form is prohibited without the prior written consent of the publisher.

LetteraVentidue Edizioni S.r.l.
Via Luigi Spagna 50 P
96100 Siracusa, Italy

www.letteraventidue.com

Gerardo Semprebon

Rural Futures

**Toward an Urban(ized) Peasantry
in the Chinese Countryside**

LetteraVentidue

Contents

Foreword

Ilaria Valente

The transition toward a lower-carbon and healthier environment is profoundly interlinked with human lifestyles and settlement forms. Within this process, the rural-urban dichotomy proved to be a fast-evolving concept that materializes with controversial modalities of territorial organizations, challenging consolidated theories and practices. China, a country with an impressive urbanization rate, is also leading experiments with new forms of ruralities, which are essential to mitigate demographic contractions and, more in general, in controlling the rural-urban material and immaterial fluxes. In this way, rural China showcases a paramount variety of approaches to countryside development, available to our observation and appreciation. In this volume, Semprebon explores some crucial ties running across people's lives and their dwelling habitat, shedding light on current spatial modification trends from an architectural and urban design perspective. A peculiar perception of the rural future emerges and identifies a new understanding of country living. In this way, his text significantly participates in an international debate that is gradually forsaking polarized positions presenting the rural and the urban as two disengaged realms. From a European perspective, looking at rural China is much more than an exercise of criticism. Semprebon describes a new fertile terrain of comparison, mutual understanding, and, perhaps, source of inspiration, even recognizing contextual distinctiveness. This is important in the current historical moment, permeated by a global crisis, which has shacked our basic assumptions about the rural-urban dichotomy.

Foreword

Ma Wenjun

Although this is an urban era where more than half of human beings live in cities, it can not survive without the countryside. As an incomplete open system, cities exchange various material and humanistic spirits with the countryside. The maintenance of rural existence and sustainable development can preserve ecological, cultural, and physical diversities, the origin of human history, or the destination of some people's life voyage. In China, the protection and revival of rural areas are also related to the success of poverty alleviation projects. However, even if the mega Rural Revitalization Strategy can get the warm support of the majority of farmers, and everyone is eager for the bright future of rural areas, there are still some prominent issues in its implementation which need to be solved as a whole and put the countryside's transformation in a multidisciplinary debate.

In Chinese tradition, no matter whether a person is successful in a political position or in a mediocre life, he always has a dream of "returning to his roots" and hopes to find his nostalgia, which includes not only the natural landscape and the village environment but also the cultural inheritance and development. With the rapid development of China's reform and opening policy since 1978, the countryside has become an old dream that can never be forgotten. The first generation of migrant workers who went out in those years is about to retire and return to their hometown. We will have to wait and see what they expect and what changes they will bring to their hometown.

Design in the Rural: China as an Experimental Field

Over the last decades, while the urban has relentlessly devoured the rural, the unsustainable extraction of resources of any kind from the farmland and unhampered spilling of pollution and waste emerged globally as crucial multidisciplinary issues. In China, while foreign observers have filled Western newspapers' pages with the outstanding numbers of national urban development, the countryside was silently reshaping its connotations[1]. This essay focuses on Chinese ruralities, considering the ongoing spatial transformations and related driving ideologies. This theme derives from two aspects. What concerns the countryside as a field of engagement is determined by my commitment to Chinese rural revitalization embarked on between 2016 and 2020 during my doctoral research. The research was jointly conducted between Milan and Shanghai - two places far culturally, beyond geographically – and placed me in the condition of reflecting on design culture, approaches, and techniques featuring the two contexts. The second aspect concerns a design-oriented spirit of observation and how it creates bridges with research. As I learned during my studies in architecture, the Latin word for designing is *pro-iectare*, which literally means "to throw forward". Observations and findings then assumed perspectives and trajectories sensible to seize potential transformations embedded within sites. Last but not least, both the Ph.D. programs of Milan and Shanghai assumed design explorations as crucial aspects of research[2], and it is not by chance that the first move into the Chinese countryside was a design proposal for the «beautification» of a village in the Fujian Province[3]. Three considerations fuel the reflections contained in this manuscript.

First, the ongoing vertiginous transformation puts rural China in a hot framework: a crossroad contested by the expectations and demands of a variety of stakeholders and actors. In regard to this, the regime of conflict well documented in several works assumes a monumental scale in the friction between economic growth, environmental stability, and cultural preservation.

Second, a growing number of cultural institutions are claiming a renovated approach to how transforming Chinese ruralities, tracing the seeds of new trajectories of development. Several forces nurture this approach, the most evident of which is envisioned in the notion of Rural Revitalization (RR). RR offers a new field of action for architectural design, where the socioeconomic and political demands can encounter with cultural and ecological aspects of rural development.

Third, the homogeneous habitats produced by global forces - mostly in urban areas – are compromising local identities, neglecting sense of place and feelings of belonging. We reached the paradoxical condition in which «today, even a "new" city is familiar: a predictable accumulation of roads, towers, icons … but as soon as we leave the urban condition behind us we confront newness and the profoundly unfamiliar»[4] as recently remarked by Rem Koolhaas. Against the backdrop of urbanization and globalization processes, the countryside becomes a source of cultural authenticity and recognition. This is particularly true in a country where rural futures are going to enshrine urban characters pervasively.

Hence, some questions have reverberated during my doctoral studies: how can architectural design tackle rural areas' extremely complex transformation? In particular, what role can play architectural design in a heterogeneous process often driven by forces numb to the site's distinctiveness? These were the destabilizing issues addressed by my research, at least at its kickstart.

As Nigel Cross well explained in the 1980s, design disciplines follow peculiar patterns of knowledge, based on the constant exploration of new techniques, new perspectives, and new horizons, which seldom can be replicated out of the context in which they are born. They struggle to find authority and legitimacy in an ever more sectorized scientific world, too far from the objectivity of measurable evidence characterizing *hard sciences*, as well as from a discourse based on historical sources, such as part of the humanities[5]. Common sense would suggest that approaches "place-based", as they claim to be in ordinary conditions, generate original – or at least diverse – outcomes. And so it was, as the variety of vernacular architecture proves in responsively responding to climate challenges, to make an example. Such a richness was created by ordinary people, integrating distinctive functional needs and cultural aspects, in most of the cases not codified yet clear and rigorous in design methods[6]. One could imply that

15

the impossibility of replicability should secure design studies and practices from disciplinary depletion, generating distinctive outcomes according to the site's specificity. Conversely, large portions of rural territories witness a progressive homogenization of forms of living, where, for instance, the Chinese countryside represents a violent battlefield and at the same time a research frontier.

Since the dramatic frictions between the urban and rural areas are far to be narrowed, remaining the main obstacle to inclusive nationwide development, Chinese authorities are swinging the spotlights on dynamics of countryside transformation. Indeed, over the last twenty years, supporting rural growth and amelioration have ranked in the top priorities in domestic policy dossiers. Design discipline flanked such an escalation, fueling burgeoning attention to complicated research agendas that struggle to combine countryside overall development with safeguarding the environment and protecting cultural legacies. In particular, the need to protect fragile heritage, whose notion has progressively expanded to include the rural as an authorized domain, produced controversial outputs, witnessing a widespread retreat of design thinking as a driver of place-making. Disneyfication practices transformed whole settlements into touristic destinations relying upon external resources; land consolidation actions removed entire hamlets to rearrange the population in dense blocks deleting inherited strata of history, and the list could go on. Nevertheless, a non-negligible movement of ambitious intellectuals imagined alternative paths to resurrect the countryside, creating the premises for flourishing design-driven processes. They assumed the rural as a new condition for exploring design innovation, transferring their vision in the global academic arena in a crucial moment of human history, namely just after the urban population's rate had overcome the symbolic threshold of 50%. Here I recall the prominent positions that emerged in the last years arriving at our present.

In 2013, in the framework of his design studio held at the Harvard Graduate School, Christopher C. M. Lee started investigating «theoretical problems and practical challenges» posed by the Chinese development model. The education and research project blossomed in a publication series also contributed by Peter G. Rowe, whose third volume focused on the «status of the countryside in the context of state-driven initiatives to urbanize rural areas»[7]. Lee led his students to radically rethink the possibilities offered by design in the context of existing Chinese policies targeted to alleviate the rural-urban socio-economic gap, which at that time considered village relocations as the primary strategy of intervention. The projects illustrated in the book explore new relationships between rural and urban living and overcome the classic antinomy by proposing innovative – some time provocative - forms of rural settlements. The title itself *Taiqian. The Countryside as a City* warns the reader about the inconsistency of existing definitions and necessity, in the author's opinion, to put forward new social and spatial models. We can read clearly how the demand for densification of the built forms, aimed at increasing and rationalizing the agricultural surface, represents a transversal feature but generates unpredictable and interesting spatial results. The notion of an urban(ized) countryside has also been proposed in the chapter "Designing for an Urban Countryside" of the book *Village in the City*, where the idea of an inextricable interpenetration of urbanities and ruralities materializes in the form of villages engulfed by cities[8].

In the same years, two publications by the group Rural Urban Framework (RUF) presented the issues of designing in the transitional context of the Chinese countryside in a straightforward and pragmatic way. They realized a sort of on-site observatory and implemented their architectural skills to play an active role against the backdrop of the massive transformations taking place on rural territories[9]. Their approach engages with local communities and includes participatory processes as the privileged means to propose significant projects, which, most of the time, envisage practices of self-construction and mutual learning. Differently from the position expressed by Christopher M. C. Lee, they address the countryside as a new – yet rural and not urban – realm, questioning the role of architecture in a context that appears not really interested in architects' contribution, as they acknowledge.

Over the last years, Bolchover, Lin, and other members of the collective continued disseminating their research and projects, actively participating in an evolving debate fostered by governance and cultural institutions. Two significant episodes pinpoint RUF influence in the current research arena, which may be identified in the 2018 participation in the Venice Architecture Biennale and the recent inclusion in the 50 best architecture firms by the magazine *Domus*. In 2016, a thematic issue of the journal *Architectural Design* entitled *Designing the Rural*, edited by Joshua Bolchover, John Lin, and Christiane Lange (RUF) integrated contributions and perspectives from all over the world, concentrating on the quest for rural development. They called for contributions and positions about the status of ruralities worldwide, provoking their contributors with the question of whether the countryside is or not just the frontline of urbanization[10].

Curiously, the call was picked up also by Patrik Schumacher, who explicitly encouraged scholars and practitioners not to waste time in the countryside. According to him

it is the new density, dynamism, diversity and synergetic complexity of big cities that challenges us and urgently requires the most advanced design resources, and not the low density and simplicity of rural communicative situations that thus pose comparatively trivial architectural problems. My thesis is that architects' attention to rural conditions is a relative waste of their precious time [...] This disadvantage of design investment in rural situations could only be compensated if very generic problems were identified and the solutions allowed for a massive generalized roll-out. But such projects are engineering-led rather than architectural

19

> [...] It will therefore become a vast engineered landscape of physical machine-based production processes, where the absence or sparseness of human life will limit the need for architectural design [...] is such investment in rural possibilities promising enough? I doubt it, because there are no real clients calling for this work[11].

Schumacher contested the invocations by contributors, labeled as ideological anti-capitalistic positions. He endorsed more businesslike approaches regulated by undisputed market dynamics, the only ones worthy of assessing social merit via profitability. His point of view underrated the growing body of institutional, cultural, and economic forces converging on rural territories. In this group, we can find political programs, such as, thinking to the Italian context, the National Strategy for Internal Areas promoted by the National Agency for Social Cohesion, which is fostering measures to boost economies in marginalized areas, including designers among the involved players. EU research funded programs are present as well, like *Ruritage, Interreg Alpine Space*, the *Smart Villages Network*, the *European Network for Rural Development*, to mention a few. Then, a turning point can be identified in the participation of China and Italy at the 16th Architecture Biennale held in Venice in 2018, with exhibitions focused on innovative design approaches in the respective countrysides. In Italy and China, we can also observe signals of a little yet symbolic trend of returning to remote areas by urban populations. It seems reasonable to predict that these demographic movements toward ruralities will gain substance with the outbreak of Covid-19 and the global re-discovery of remote working. In China, for instance, the growing demand by domestic tourism for rural destinations is symptomatic of progressive urban alienation and intolerance. This escape from large cities may anticipate a more radical social structure shift where small and medium-size rural settlements like county-level towns could gain attractiveness by conveying urban standards in rural areas. Such interest has political and economic implications that can not be neglected. *Beautiful Villages. Rural Construction Practice in Contemporary China*[12], together with the coeval *Building a Future Countryside*[13] and *Rural Moves. The Songyang Story*[14] are books portraying a vibrant panorama of architectural projects that are reshaping a new rural self-awareness. Introducing the Chinese exhibition at the Venice Biennale, Hans-Jorgen Commerell, Director of Aedes Architecture Forum in Berlin, acknowledged the momentum reached by designing in the rural in China but, at the same time, warned us on the threats embedded in countryside development, such as rural identity jeopardized by massive tourism or the disneyfication of the exotic above-mentioned[15].

Other significant experiences in rural development are the renowned realizations by Zhang Lei and Wang Shu – to quote two star architects – or the rural utopia imagined in Bishan by activist Ou Ning[16], which represents one of the most fortunate cases of grassroots engagement. In this group, a remarkable and successful experience is the revitalization of the Songyang

County in the Zhejiang Province through "architectural acupuncture" orchestrated by Xu Tiantian, one of the protagonists of this vanguard architect movement experimenting with design in the countryside. She remarked that

> with the intention to re-calibrate the relationship between the urban and the countryside, our engagement was not only to address the economic and ecological impacts of urbanization but on a conceptual level, offer a new vision through architectural practices. Architecture is not an end or a final product, but rather the means to transform and to instigate change[17].

These experiments manifested the complexity – and sometimes contradictions – of rural development, which remains an affair going far beyond the domain of solely architectural design. From one side, architects demonstrated their eagerness to participate in rural reconstruction, a tangible, but perhaps mainly cultural, fact. On the other side, the countryside has taught designers and planners the richness and variety of rural values, knowledge, wisdom, and aesthetics by bringing to light the fragile roots of Chinese society. This double-directional process proves the necessity for a more intense interplay between the subject operator agencies and object operated, the rural, which remains a significant tank of capital, ideas, and people. In particular, the projects exposed at the Biennale of Venice in 2018 revealed how architectural design could ponder profoundly on contextual relationships, generating positive externalities on the surrounding built fabric. These examples challenged the collective consciousness by questioning whether or not there was a chance to be contemporary and to be rural without chasing urban models. This point captures our interest: is the urban an appropriate source of methods and ideas to be re-elaborated, not to say transferred, in the rural, or should designers practicing in the rural search for inspiration - and legitimation – elsewhere, such as the rural itself? We do not question the virtue of transcultural and cross boundaries contaminations that have historically, in most cases, raised the bar of practitioners; instead, we ponder on the contemporary architectural condition of the rural, by-passing any idealistic dimension of the project.

The core aspect moving the reflections in this book addresses the relationships materializing between place-making and design, questioning the capability to deliver valuable solutions - and knowledge - on uses and forms for life. I went into the deep countryside with this spirit to explore unbiased realities – after observing those a little bit romanticized on architectural magazines - trying to seize their dynamics of change and related design approaches. The forms of rural territories appeared in all their fascinating and conflicting nature, exposing a complex and layered substratum too malleable to resist societal changes and economic impulses. Impotent in front of globalizing modernity, only a few fragments of traditional China stubbornly survived the spreading of new social and spatial paradigms. Notwithstanding, I myself experienced the cultural vitality of traditional buildings, especially family and deity temples that, far from being fetishized relics of a lost time, proved to play a fundamental role in rural society and the built environment without losing meanings and functions. At the same time, I found that the concretization of pilot, demonstration, ideal settlement models is forging the foundations for a rural *saga* that is already praised and claimed by authorities. Thus we need to ask what is the role of a design if we repudiate tasks that are utilitarian to such heroic narration and, at the same time, any idealistic or autonomous dimension. The question opens space for a debate not really interested in absolute responses detached from contextual specifications. We can say that design, to play in coherency with a state of necessity, needs to formulate the compelling questions before conveying optimized solutions, challenging habits and common practices if necessary.

In regard to this, Rem Koolhaas draw the architectural community's attention to the condition of ruralities, claiming that «the countryside is largely off (our) radar, an "ignored realm"» and inviting his readers to reconsider the potential embedded in marginalized territories. For him, «the inevitability of Total Urbanization must be questioned, and the countryside must be rediscovered as a place to stay alive; enthusiastic human presence must reanimate it with new imagination»[18]. His inquiry is presented in the form of a report compiled by researchers practicing in different parts of the world, portraying an updated and composite picture of the rural.

Toward the end of 2019, while visiting the Beijing Advanced Innovation Center for Future Urban Design of Beijing University of Civil Engineering and Architecture (BUCEA), I interviewed Sun Zhe, professor and expert in grassroots practice for countryside development, about the future of Chinese rural areas. In his opinion, rural areas had tremendous spatial potential, especially in the post-industrial era, by providing various services to supplement the city's inadequate functions. For him, an architect who wanted to play an effective role in the countryside had to adapt to multiple identities. He claimed the architect could be a synthesis of a sociologist, a villager, and a designer. For Sun Zhe, architecture could be envisioned as a driver for rural development because, as he told me «it has to pass through to adaptation of physical space, which must involve architecture. Architecture here must be an interdisciplinary discipline. Why not? It has been evolving over time!»[19].

These clues represent just the most visible part of a more structural mobilization that sees different agencies concentrating on ruralities as a renovated field of engagement for design-driven research. Among these, China's political commitment to realizing an Ecological Civilization (EC), a goal recently inscribed in the Party's constitution, represents a decisive move forward and places the countryside in a delicate predicament, hostage of an epic narration, sometimes inflated, and dessert on a silver plate for a land-use authorized transition. Nevertheless, such a mobilization represents the current occasion to rethink the countryside encompassing rural's basic assumption and ultimate implications, which can be synthesized in the relationships with urban centers.

Explaining their approach to design, Bolchover, Lin, and Lange affirmed that «there is no delineation between research and design - realizing a project itself creates questions. Construction is only the beginning of testing our hypotheses as to how the project and its context will evolve»[20]. This intellectual bridge looks appropriate to generate those promising alliances between users and solution-givers interested in addressing the problems characterizing rural territories. Perhaps, this bridge, beyond re-activating that fruitful double directional process mentioned above, is likely to deliver alternative ways to frame the problems by defining new challenges and opening parallel perspectives. One of these challenges was the primary attempt of my doctoral research. It questioned the possibility by design disciplines to critically frame the transient and controversial condition of the Chinese countryside by considering an ordinary - but representative of a multitude - case study. Indeed, these reflections moved from a practical necessity addressed in my research, whose first act was the design proposal of a new settlement layout for the village itself. Following the routine practice of land consolidation, the village was destined to be almost wholly demolished and rebuilt to ensure more rational use of the space, particularly for intensive agricultural purposes. The bucolic plain surrounded by green hills, which hosts Zhangyang, was likely to become an enormous working site. My first bewilderment became an awareness as I visited other neighborhoods recently realized in the nearby, like a «Happy Community of the New Countryside», where I found a high-dense housing district organized on a rigid urban-like grid, presented as a successful model of rural development. When I joined the SJTU-Polimi Sino-Italian research team, Zhangyang village had recently applied to be enlisted as a demonstration project of "countryside beautification". Moving across the boundaries of academic and practice contexts, I observed the development process with the purpose of exploring an alternative path of transformation.

The second chapter of the book introduces the Chinese peasantry's evolved condition, characterized by the accepted vision portraying rural futures with urban connotations. The urbanization of the rural has been repeatedly invoked as a panacea, alternatively labeled as rural-urban integration, villages' "townization", or a new type of urbanization. The crucial challenge appears to prefigure how the floating population of migrant workers will find a legitimated and acknowledged social status in their living place, allowing their accommodation to affect settlements outside big cities positively.

The third chapter reflects on the observations that emerged during fieldwork. I selected the cases of Zhangyang and Jiankou as paradigmatic cases of a transitional condition. Indeed, they respectively show evidence of, from one side, a settlement spontaneously raised as the aggregation of four natural villages which – despite still in expansion - risks to be canceled and rebuilt more compactly; on the other side, a settlement which has just experienced such a transformation. I tried to turn the «intellectual disorientation» mentioned by Jullien, a feeling typically suffered by foreign observers, into an unbiased attitude to objectively read the phenomenology of territories via the direct observation of their form, built and non-built[21].

This manuscript concludes by recalling those driving ideologies and conceptual apparatus that are regulating the development of rural China. The massive and irreversible transformations mentioned above were envisioned by strategies, plans, and projects inscribed in an authorized domain. In China, despite difficulties and contradictions, a new awareness is emerging, which can be stigmatized in the concepts of *Building a Moderately Prosperous Society, Rural Revitalization* (RR*)* and *Ecological Civilization* (EC). The momentum reached by these notions is reshaping the cultural dimension of Chinese rural development, and within it and designing in the rural, placing them in a vanguard position compared to global trends of countryside transformations, as Rem Koolhaas declared on the occasion of the exhibition at the Solomon R. Guggenheim Museum. This is why, as remarked by the father of the concept of EC, John B. Bobb, «China's official goal of ecological civilization could become the global goal. Real, urgently needed, changes could be made»[22].

New common grounds are being forged, where different forces – cultural, political, and economic - are mobilized to shape a future and peculiar condition of the countryside. It is expected that the next stage of the global countryside will probably be related and affected by Chinese achievements or failures in rural development. In this scenario, Beijing will play a leading role in pushing forward a new ideal of rurality and open inescapable perspectives for international observers.

Migrant Workers: a Chance to Rethink Rural and Urban Status

It took them another fifteen minutes, however, before the village came in view. There was a striking discrepancy between the kinds of houses clustered there. Some were new, modern, substantial, like mansions in the best area of Shanghai, but others were old, shabby, and small. «It's like two different worlds here,» Yu observed. «Exactly,» Zhao said. «There's a huge gap between households with people abroad and those without. All these new houses have been built with money sent from overseas.» «It's amazing. These new houses would be worth millions on Shanghai.» «Let me give you some numbers, Detective Yu. A peasant's yearly income here is around three thousand Yuan, and that depends on the weather. Some in New York can earn that sum in a week – living, eating, sleeping in a restaurant, and getting paid all in cash. One year's savings there is enough to pay for a two-story house here, full of new furniture and appliance, too. How can families without people abroad compete? They have to remain huddled in those ancient huts, in the shadow of the upstarts»[1].

On their way to a rural village in the Fujian Province, agents Yu and Zhao discuss the huge discrepancy in housing conditions, addressing the reasons for such a gap to the gains earned by migrant workers who decide to work far from their hometown. In this dialogue taken from the novel *A Loyal Character Dancer*, Qiu Xiaolong portrays a sharp picture of the extreme conditions featuring the Chinese countryside at the beginning of the 1990s when migration flows were already reshaping the socioeconomic pattern of ruralities dramatically[2].

Despite the central government's efforts to lift out of poverty the national population within 2020 and mitigate the rural-urban gap[3], China suffers from striking socioeconomic disparities, whose main drivers remain society's dual structure[4]. The anthropologist Bryan Tilt, who conducted ten years of fieldwork in South West rural China, portrayed such imparity with these words.

I have often reflected that I experience less culture shock when I get off the airplane from the west coast of the United States to Beijing than I do when I board a train or a bus and travel from the city into the Chinese countryside[5].

The issue of migrant workers, which is barycentric in the disparities between urban and rural, is substantially determined by the rigid social divide generated by the *hukou* system, which is the national Household Registration System. Indeed, the migrant workers are rural-recorded citizens working in a city. The *hukou* divides the population into two categories: rural residents working in the first sector and citizens working in the second sector. These two groups, rural and urban recorded citizens, enjoy different rights not interchangeable. The system was conceived in the Maoist era to plan the use of public resources and services. Nevertheless, what was supposed to guarantee equal or comparable standards among citizens, has stimulated dramatic disparities. Indeed, beyond hampering inclusiveness (especially in cities), the *hukou* resulted in a growing gap of revenues and living standards between the urban and the rural population, realizing the structural premises for class segregation[6]. Even though the *hukou* system has been considerably altered, the government still uses it to plan expenses for social services. In particular, the *hukou* prevents peasants from accessing the rights and services granted to urban residents in cities, such as education for children, health care assistance, and legally buying a house's use right[7].

Since the late 1970s, the pursuit of more remunerative jobs induced the youngest family members to commute or migrate to urban areas. Some manage to properly integrate into cities by starting new economic enterprises, attending education training, or following other social inclusion programs. The majority struggle to get an urban *hukou* and becomes part of the enormous floating population, counting hundreds of million citizens, named migrant workers, a category of people with anything but their labor force that moves from place to place or travels back and forth between the registered residence and the workplace[8].

Migrant workers receive inferior treatment and discrimination and can not access the common urban welfare. They lay «in a state of limbo»[9], legally restricted to the countryside rules by the *hukou* registration, yet economically dependent on the city. The World Bank report on China specifies that

> the majority of migrant workers are male, and on average they are better educated than the general rural labor force [and] the average migrant worker stays in the city for only seven to nine years, and only 20 percent of migrants have brought their families, although more than 50 percent would like to settle in urban areas[10].

For Reng Xiang migrant workers represent a slice of the population living at the periphery, «both geographically and mentally, struggling through their lives in this national play about land and rights»[11]. Urban citizens consider migrant workers as uncultured, backward ad less civilized peasants, putting them in a subaltern condition, which is the social premise for discrimination and even segregation. In the countryside as well, migrants happen to be frowned upon since their lifestyles are incompatible with the traditional family structure, according to which a family has «four generations under one roof». Indeed breaking with traditions in a context where secular habits are highly considered causes additional disapproval. In the name of urban industrial growth, the socioeconomic burden inherited by the *hukou* has impacted generations of peasants, relegating them to pre-determined existences, inhibiting personal talents and attitudes, crushing hopes and efforts, shaping dreams and aspirations, dooming lives to farming dependence to survive. On the other side of the (dis)equation, the socialist state reserved a parcel of land for villagers, performing as a sort of personal reservoir for basic needs. For migrant workers, it became the last resource, in case of ill-fortune in cities, and the decisive reluctance to break linkages with rural homeplaces. Giuliano Marrucci, an Italian television reporter, defined this aspect as the «sunny side of *hukou*», tracing within it the ultimate form of salvation. After the crisis of 2009, millions of migrant workers lost their occupations in the city.

They fell back on the countryside, where they found little pieces of land assigned for cultivation and housing construction. Surprisingly, he disclosed that, in a national survey conducted in 2010 across 106 cities, only 26% of migrants would have changed their rural *hukou* into an urban one, realizing the protection role played by a rural *hukou*[12]. Nevertheless, as remarked by the World Bank, the rural-urban divide has brought inherent disparities in public safety, human healthcare, economic disparities, and social instability.

China's urbanization over the last three decades has been unprecedented in scale: 260 million migrants have moved to cities from rural areas, supporting the country's rapid economic growth and development progress. Despite the enormity of this transition, China has avoided some of the ills often associated with urbanization, particularly large-scale urban poverty and unemployment. But strains have begun to emerge in the form of rising inequality, environmental degradation, and the quickening depletion of natural resources[13].

Migrant workers have secured urban areas an incessant and interchangeable labor force at low prices, becoming *de facto* the country's main productive force, available at cheap costs and deprived of social welfare. At the same time, they also provoked two negative externalities on countryside territories. On the one hand, the so-called rural exodus contributed to the loss of human capital from rural areas, weakening an already stagnant economy. In a system regulated on children and elderlies' demands, cramped space remained for

35

strengthening entrepreneurial innovation and the service sector in general. On the other hand, the jobs in the cities provided rural citizens the financial resources to build new houses in the home village. The new dwellings, which were usually oversized to host all the family members that gather during festivals and holidays, became one of the primary thrusts causing the alteration of rural territories[14.]

Strictly related to the issue of migrant workers are, indeed, the processes of spontaneous – and sometimes informal – construction, issues pairing the global problem of "village hollowing". In China, the notion emerged in the early 1990s as a phenomenon embodying three essential features: a loss of land resources in rural areas due to housing expansion, a decrease of rural population due to outflowing migrations, the realization of new houses, and simultaneous abandonment of old, dilapidated ones. Village hollowing's driving forces embody many heterogeneous factors, including economic, socio-cultural, institutional-managerial, and environmental ones. The scarce agricultural modernization negatively impacted farming productivity, turning croplands located in the fringe areas of villages into attractive tanks of land available for housing construction, rather than agricultural purposes, which appeared to be less profitable uses. Peasants moved into the newly built dwellings, leaving vacant the old ones at the centers of villages. Another factor performing as a decisive driver for the discrepancy between the rural resident population and the rural housing stock is «seasonal vacancy» or absenteeism due to migrant workers living in cities.

The existing system of land ownership prevented free trade of rural houses without clarifying what had to be done of the land when the household migrated either temporally or permanently. Rural land, which belonged to village cooperatives, could only be transferred to other community members or authorities, such as the government in turn of compensation, often unbalanced but necessary to Chinese larger end to urbanize[15]. The local governments boosted market mechanisms, attracting financial forces to invest in rural development, passing through village demolition and reconstruction, as well as people relocation. Despite sometimes resorting to coercive practices, rural urbanization has increasingly been considered the main driver for enhancing people's conditions by generating a new population of urban(ized) peasantry.

We have to place this oxymoron notion in its socio-cultural trajectory to seize its extent and deepness. In the early 1980s, the Chinese population was 80% rural. All the indicators have shown the vertiginous path of demographic urbanization despite the mitigation role played by the still in force *hukou* system. The current dynamics of countryside development reflect responsively the evolving patterns of Chinese societal and economic conditions, which, with dramatic disparities, are generally ameliorating[16]. The crucial point is that the shrinking of the rural population was not only due to the hemorrhage of peasants moving to urban areas. A large slice of the rural registered population was urbanized just as part of a broader plan for building a modern urban China by structurally reorganizing countless settlements in the countryside, including villages' demolition and reconstructions in the forms of denser neighborhoods. According to the government official statistics, the integration of urban and rural development has taken a new step. In terms of numbers, between 2012 and 2017, more than eighty million agricultural migrants have become urban residents, with a pace of sixteen million people per year flow[17]. The decrease of peasants recorded people has been therefore in line with the plan, announced in 2005 by the Chinese government to urbanize 350 million rural citizens by 2030, determining the most massive migrations ever. In Prime Minister Li Keqiang National Plan for New Urbanization for 2020, peasants' urbanization was not equal everywhere. Big cities were supposed to accept trained rural citizens, especially in technical or scientific, while cities with a population lower of one million people had to include the majority without peculiar distinction.

Toward the end of 2020, President Xi Jinping declared that China successfully eradicated extreme poverty. Even though such a proclamation may enshrine rhetoric accents and many observers are skeptical about its effectiveness, signals of massive improvements are evident, especially compared to previous decades. The construction of a pharaonic infrastructural network, still in progress, is securing the population the possibility of movements across the country and, at the same time, fueling the phenomenon of migrant workers.

Rural-urban outflow migrations exacerbated problems related to the transition of agricultural land use. A vast literature has investigated patterns and intensities of this multifaceted and georeferenced issue. An aspect making this transition hot was that Chinese food security and autarchy could be threatened by the mentioned agricultural change since change usually corresponded with loss. Lester Brown raised this point already 25 years ago, bringing on Beijing's agenda the severe numbers of Chinese demographic and agricultural conditions. In his book *Who will feed China,* he wondered how more than 21% of the world population would have relied on 7% of world cultivated land without planning drastic mitigation measures[18]. Chinese urbanization rush was evident even then, and history tells us that policy-makers did not question it; indeed, they pushed and regulated it using the most powerful instrument in the governments' hands: the *hukou*, sided by a persuasive narration of the countryside urbanization, which assumed epic tones, overturning centuries of rural supremacy.

Some will read an ironic twist of fate in the numerous urban research trends exploring ways of reintroducing farming production within cities as well as strident and caricatural representations of nature staged in concrete and steel jungles that resonate as insults to injuries. Let's the urban do the urban and the rural do the rural one could argue, but this is not conceivable in a vision solely urban-oriented. Thus, conciliating the rural and the urban or accommodating the rural in the urban remains a desirable, if not obliged, option.

This provocation helps us to observe the countryside with critical eyes, detecting its dramatic problems but also its, at this point priceless, potentials embedded in its long-lasting historical trajectory and privileged relationships with environmental resources. In this game, migrant workers play a fundamental role that regards architectural and urban design too, since a peculiar built environment will have to accommodate migrants decently.

For decades, this floating population has served as the primary labor force source, performing as the industrial engine's propellant that fueled the Chinese economic rise. Even though the uneven distribution of resources generated impressive and structural asymmetries between rural and urban worlds, the constant, yet sometimes imperceptible, improvement mitigated the social tensions tied to the opaque distribution of rights. Making the rural more similar to the urban was not only the easiest way to rationalize land uses by relocating and concentrating entire villages but also represented the evocative provision of the promised heaven directly at the peasants' homeplace. On one side, the denser and urban-like anonymous towns born from *tabula rasa* constructions - which will be introduced in the next chapter - presented as the purified and healthy versions of cities, became the hegemonic spatial paradigm. This "townization" conjugated the distribution of basic services to the weaker sectors of the population with the imperatives of industrial growth and grain production. On the other side, the frenetic building of detached villas in remote villages, often realized without formal projects or plannings, was allowed in light of synergies between weak governances and private initiatives. These accidental alliances created the schizophrenic premises to carelessly alter villages' spatial characters, especially in fringe areas, generating inefficient land uses and cultural losses.

An aspect is traceable in both mentioned transformation routes, top-down and bottom-up: rural settlements are losing the countryside spatialities, mostly by dismantling the structural and historical link between housing and farming space. To reduce rural-urban gaps, peasants are acquiring urban connotations, starting from their domestic reality but including forms of collectivity, with their spatial implications as well. An ideological method can be inferred, which see in the introduction of urban simulacra in the countryside, the attempt of solving - perhaps in some case hiding - the rural problems. There is no reason to contest such a process *per se*, especially considering the will to flatten inequalities and simultaneously stem demographic outflows. Nevertheless, top-down townization and bottom-up construction as standard practices of rural development revealed a multitude of problems that are shacking the cultural and environmental dimensions of Chinese ruralities. Therefore, migrants' integration and communities' resettlement call for aware and pro-active commitments of design disciplines to accommodate the new urban(ized) peasantry.

A Journey through Ordinary Practices of Rural Development

The Chinese's rush to rural urbanization grafts market mechanisms on a socialist society. Central and local governments move in a State Capitalism system to increase the economic productivity of the land[1]. In the countryside, both top-down and bottom-up development processes are taking place. During my fieldwork, I encountered these two development routes, planned top-down and unplanned bottom-up, representing the primary paths of rural urbanization. They are the offspring of two political seasons: the 1970s-1990s market-oriented openings, and the 2000s-2010s planned programs. Both cases here presented regard villages located in the administrative jurisdiction of Hanjiang District, Putian City, Fujian Province. The first is Jiankou Village, a recently realized neighborhood that was presented to my eyes as a virtuous example of rural development resulting from policy implementation. The second case is Zhangyang Village, the rural settlement assumed as the case study of my doctoral research.

My first visit to Jiankou village was in August 2017. The settlement was a new housing neighborhood resulting from the demolition of an existing natural village. The driving concept was to optimize the land's productivity, against the backdrop of the recent policies known as *Building a New Socialist Countryside*, *Increasing Urban Construction Land by Decreasing Rural Construction Land*, and *Implementing the New-type Urbanization*. In the village's public hall, the program's goals and principal design phases were documented on exhibition panels.

Jiankou Village [...] was once a little-known remote village. Since it was included in the pilot project for the «Happy Communities» in 2012, the community started from 'dismantling the old village and building the new one,' and worked to transform the settlement in a 'happy dwelling place in a mountainous area, with an agricultural park and a central village' that combines liveable environment, ecological agriculture, and farmland sightseeing. [...] it enhances the integration between industries and villages, mobilizing rural resources, and helping farmers to get rich.

From one side, I realized that the project optimized the spatial layout providing a relatively large and cost-effective amount of services. Indeed, the village could praise different achievements like the consolidation of more than 80.000 sqm of arable land; the supply to 194 new dwellings, equipped with modern amenities; the realization of infrastructural networks; the introduction of new industries. On the other side, the new compact fabric introduced a small-town atmosphere, replacing the former settlement whose layered morphologies were canceled according to a *tabula rasa* method. A rigid grid organized the built form generating repeated arrays of redundant middle-rise row houses equipped with little gardens in front of the main dwelling's entrance, reinforcing a pseudo urban image.

The built form was determined via functional zoning - almost entirely housing - substantially indifferent to contextual specificities and featuring a character of atopy. At the scale of architecture, the aesthetic values appeared trivial and reduced to a questionable apparatus of decorations applied on banal buildings. A pseudo urban environment without the cities' complexity and stratification was created by repeating ubiquitously a few building types on a rigid grid-based layout. It was evident that engineering-like mechanisms, implemented to maximize the value of rural surfaces, had driven the configuration of the new settlement, as similarly described by Lee:

> The strategic purpose of these new towns follows from the ambitions set out in the New Socialist Countryside. First, they safeguard agricultural land and make it more efficient by combining fragmented farming areas, entailing the demolition of villages deemed to be inefficiently located or laid out. Second, they aim to improve the living conditions in the villages by building new structures, doing away with the cumbersome process of inserting and upgrading existing villages with basic sanitation and energy, amenities, and housing stock. Third, they increase the GDP of the villages by making agriculture more efficient and mechanized and by promoting the introduction of small commercial streets with workshops, retail, restaurants, and small markets. Finally, with the increased GDP and the improved conditions, they make the villages viable again, stemming the flow of rural migrants to the cities[2].

Jiankou Village represented a paradigmatic case of rural development ordinary practices, whose implementation modalities entered the scientific literature[3]. From the project outcomes, one can infer the struggle by design to play a critical role without limiting itself to blindly translating the program goals into generic volumes. The systematic replica of this formula makes it, *de facto*, the standard implementation mode in rural

45

development. Nevertheless, and paradoxically, this *tabula rasa* approach encapsulated spatial characters distinctively Chinese, nowhere to be found in other parts of the world, that generated «no longer clearly urban or rural areas, but a blending of the two»[4]. Visiting Jiankou Village raised the problematic nature of the countryside's restructuring programs, where the same forces stimulating the development, at the same time, threatened rural distinctiveness.

The second case presented is Zhangyang Village, a settlement that resulted from a long-lasting and still in progress bottom-up informal development. During the fieldwork, I tried to use architectural tools as diagnostic instruments to detect problems and possibilities inherent to the spatial conditions generated by private-driven housing construction. By observing spatial forms, uses, and, more in general, human behaviors as the primary sources of investigation, I detected a complex socioeconomic stratification that animated and gave shape to the diversified habitat. The built form blended architectural elements inherited from the past and modern ones, determining a bizarre patchwork of shapes, which later I discover to be recurrent in South-Eastern coastal regions. My impressions found correspondences with Bolchover and Lin's description:

> the village reveals many sites for new construction. Concrete foundations, piles of red bricks, and half-finished tiled houses grow like mushrooms between yellow loam pig stalls, traditional green brick courtyard houses, and ancient

ancestral halls. Some people live in dilapidated courtyard houses without electricity and water, whereas others have built four-story houses decorated with Romanesque arches and Greek-style loggias, and are provided with TV and Internet access. Some old houses and ancestral halls are left empty or used for chicken coops and storage while rice paddies are taken over by construction[5].

This picture fitted perfectly with the current condition of Zhangyang Village, a settlement in motion despite the stagnant economy, the absence of services and job opportunities, and the outflow of young people. The village's precarious conditions were readable in the grotesque landscape composed of ruins' fragments, damaged buildings, new villas, and several working sites. The migration of peasants towards big cities was causing demographic contraction and farmland shrinkage due to the expansion of housing surfaces. Indeed, the revenues guaranteed by the Household Responsibility System – a measure introduced in the early 1980s that made peasants responsible for gains and losses deriving from their farming activity - were employed in housing enlargement or construction. In consequence of that measure, spontaneous and informal urbanization processes started, like in Zhangyang, without the direction of overall planning[6]. As reported by Knapp and Dongqi:

Designs have been solicited via provincial and national competitions and popularized in countless plan books and manuals. The pace and quality of planning, however, have generally been inadequate to meet the varied demands in the countryside, and the indiscriminate occupation of farm-land continues to be a problem as village and town sites expand in an unplanned manner[7].

Beyond the economic transition started with the Reform and Opening-Up policies, another impulse for bottom-up urbanization situated in the shifting patterns of the families' composition or, using the words by Yan, the «triumph of conjugality over patriarchy»[8]. Familiar nuclei have become smaller and have celebrated privacy as the principal achievement as well as a means of emancipation[9], stimulating the construction of detached dwellings, which mushroomed on the territory. Gradually, the old houses accommodating clans became the oppressive and backward place from which to move out as soon as the finances made it possible, exacerbating the already robust rural-out migrations and informal housing constructions. It is possible to recognize two expansion patterns from the satellite images, a spot one and a diffusive one, both associated with specific buildings typologies.

The first corresponded with the construction, or replacement, of single buildings located in the denser built fabric. Due to the limitation of free space, the new houses were erected in the interstitial spaces. The spot pattern adopted typologies compatible with the existing row houses, usually two floors high, creating a spatial continuity given by seamless façades and a direct relationship between interior and exterior. The spot pattern conflicted with the "village hollowing" phenomenon since it expressed farmers' reluctance to abandon their dwellings in favor of modern villas. Even though the spot pattern did not significantly alter the urban fabric, the built space density increased either in replacement and volumetric addition cases.

The diffusive pattern, usually located in the village's fringe areas, was defined by the scattered addition of freestanding houses. The buildings were distributed freely on the land and followed the logic of "the best view in the landscape", determining irregular distances between buildings and random orientations. The new villas irremediably lost the historical and structural spatial relationship with the ground: a link that has indissolubly connected domestic and farming spaces until the rise of modern lifestyles. New dwellings laid in the middle of private yards surrounded by concrete walls, introducing *de facto* an additional degree of spatial fragmentation. Inside the walled and concrete paved yards, those isolated open spaces became the new microcosms where family life was staged. In parallel, technological, economic, and social evolutions blossomed out in the assimilation of new housing schemes, often adapted to the demands and values imported from the "modern" West. Knapp designated these freestanding multi-floor houses surrounded by a private yard with the neologism «boxlike villa». As remarked by Yan:

> Traditional dwellings and spatial arrangements, however, were largely swept away during a wave of house construction and remodeling that started in the mid-1980s, and by the late 1990s villagers were competing with one another in

49

adopting «modern» house designs. New notions of intimacy and privacy began to emerge as important concerns in family life as individuals began to have their own private lives inside the house. As a result, the home has changed from being a corporate structure to a private haven[10].

The diffusive pattern altered the built form dramatically faster than the spot one, determining the massive loss of arable land, the impairment of the settlement's formal structure, and its (past) charming image. As in many other villages in Zhangyang, the dreams of emancipating from the traditional humble living culture led householders to adapt their dwelling's image. Combining traditional symbols with exotic forms, they expressed a folkloristic attachment to their native place and an eagerness to copy from the idealized "modern" West. The free-standing multi-story residential building decorated with classical and baroque elements was spontaneously elected to express a social or economic rise and proliferated, presenting little variations on the same repeated model. With their cosmetic facades and fancy tympanums, the boxlike villas represented the typical contemporary rural multi-stories dwelling.

A conspicuous number of households felt the necessity of raising their - in most cases already tall - residence of one floor. They replicated a specific construction method without relevant variations, using panels covered with metal sheets assembled on a metal frame laid on the existing building roof. This vertical growth, coupled with the horizontal one, profoundly altered the settlement's appearance and spatial structure. The assimilation of unprecedented scales of values by peasantry reflected on the architectural (self) expression. With their homogeneity and indifference to the context, these spontaneous initiatives emphasized what can be empirically defined as a narrow architectural alphabet, both in terms of spatial organization and expressive language, determining a pervasive transformation of landscapes, physical and cultural. On the one hand, such a palpable transformation is symptomatic of a gained financial prosperity, while, on the other hand, it is flattening cultural diversities, eroding variegated forms of heritage.

Nevertheless, since 2014 the development of Zhangyang was situated in a Province-driven program conceived as a long-term path toward rural restructuring. In 2015, the Fujian Province Village Town Construction Development Center, a local state-owned enterprise (SOE) drew up the village's planning, defining goals, modalities, and forms of the project. The document included several elements. Its legal framework clarified the program position in relation to the central, Provincial, and Municipal regulations as well as the contextual planning for the District and the County. The document listed the project's generalities, like the scope, the period, the expectations, and the guiding principles.

The document contained the detailed implementation modalities, including the existing condition, the new land-use plan, the infrastructural plan, the structural retrofitting, and the short-term village's transformation. According to the planning prospect, the driving principles were the land consolidation to optimize local farming techniques and productions and implement a service industry able to inject new life in the current narrow economy. The expansion of the construction land had to meet the village population's expected increment, which from 1426 people was supposed to reach 1500 in 2020 and 1600 in 2030. The planning's main features included massive demolitions and rebuilding with higher construction indexes, generating an increased fabric density. The project provided new infrastructures and facilities, proposed multiple retrofitting, seismic, energetic, sanitary, and functional. Beyond strengthening the farming industry, the goal was to introduce new economic sectors, notably crafting and tourism. The design report claimed more space between the buildings in response to the difficulty of adding houses in the interstitial spaces. Demolitions and reconstructions had to start from the village's central area and conforming to a rigid grid-based layout. The final image had to produce a «unified style». The newly built fabric was drawn over the same sediment of demolished buildings, rectifying irregularities and concentrating the volume in rows of bi-familiar villas, sometimes detached. The rendering reproduced the similar little town atmosphere seen in other compounds recently realized.

In this case, too, emerges unquestionable positive externalities related to a general improvement of living conditions, but disciplinary design problems appeared as well. First, the number of demolitions was so high that it could not meet acceptable criteria of sustainability. Second, even assuming the total demolition as a necessary action, the repetition of the antecedent spatial configuration appeared to be pointless. There was no convincing reason to realize the new buildings in the same position and with almost the same orientation as the old ones, which resulted from spontaneous initiatives. Curiously, the planning did not include the design of one recognizable public space for shared activities able to meet current demands and adapt to future ones. Third, the project proposed to replicate *ad libitum* three housing typologies, generating a built form redundant in its architectural connotations and apparently insensible to the site's distinctiveness. The middle-rise buildings were furnished with little gardens in front of the main entrance and exhibited an awkward combination of traditional and exotic decoration, similarly to the above-mentioned boxlike villas. The ancient buildings appeared, by the rendering, rebuilt with the same forms but modern materials according to a style reconstruction.

In 2017 Zhangyang Village's authorities started a consultation process with the Shanghai Jiao Tong University, in partnership with the Politecnico di Milano, to work out an alternative plan guiding the village's development[11]. The interactions between local authorities and research groups were aligned with the benchmarks of the Strategic Plan for Rural Revitalization

53

2018-2022 which encouraged the realization of demonstrative projects as well as cooperation with scientific institutions. Zhangyang obtained the possibility of revising the planning to be enlisted as a pilot project without substantially altering the old plan's vocations, namely to become a service hub integrating leisure activities and technological innovation. The pilot project for Zhangyang Village was situated in the larger plan to make the Fujian Province one of the experimental zones with demonstrative purposes[12]. A new approach to development was put in practice since then, deviating from the *tabula rasa* method envisioned before. Villagers were consulted by fielding practices of listening and grassroots proposals. I had the chance to survey the peasants' needs and aspirations using a questionnaire answered by 99 families. Works of reparation began from securing the river banks, and the development is still in progress.

Some elements of comparison between top-down and bottom-up practices of development, which are paradigmatic for rural China, can be remarked. On the one hand, in Zhangyang, the architectural characters of dwellings have evolved spontaneously towards stile homologation, via the grotesque contamination of local symbols with Western scraps, originating a bizarre formal alphabet replicated haphazardly. Nevertheless, some original characters of the settlement morphology and fragments of historical buildings survived. Such elements reverberated traditional forms of rural lives traceable within famous Chinese Classics, paintings, poetry, and writing in general. In particular, fifteen complexes of buildings were revealed to play a fundamental role in resisting the pressure of spontaneous constructions[13]. Their spatial principles concentrated in a few formal aggregations and persisted over the last decades in the malleable rural patterns, making such buildings the physical carrier of local traditions. These vernacular architectures, whose function went beyond practical uses – they were ancestral halls and family temples - proved to be resilient elements. Like matrices, they characterized the built fabric morphology and, even though these vernacular buildings appeared suffocated by the waves of recent urbanizations, their presence suggested a non-written system of morphological rules impressed in the built texture. The spatial sequence from the altar chamber to the front yard accepted partial alterations, such as demolitions, additions, and contaminations functional to evolving lifestyles, without compromising the overall configuration[14]. Such rules and invariants entwined inextricably with the topography and deeply permeated the local physical and cultural landscape.

On the other hand, the case of Jiankou suggested that land-use optimization enhanced the services' quality, but at the same time threatened the aesthetic and cultural values that permeated the rural settlements[15]. Design disciplines gave a marginal contribution in place-making, retreating in front of tested land consolidation methodologies, based more on quantitative mechanisms than critical discernment and creative thinking[16]. The 2014 development project for Zhangyang formalized by the local SOE contained all the seeds traceable in Jiankou's new neighborhood. Both top-down planned developments expressed the problematic condition of design, relegated to serve pre-determined zoning plans and acritically supply to housing demands. The outcomes resonated as the direct application of the existing regulations without a distinctive spatial concept, as remarked by Dingliang Yang observing the effects of the *Building a New Socialist Countryside* campaign, according to who:

Designed by local architecture institutes, the houses were affordable and efficient, with living and dining areas and a semi-outdoor parking space on the first floor and two bedrooms and a terrace on each of the second and third floors. But their appearance was banal, unsuccessfully imitating, and oversimplifying, features of the traditional Chinese vernacular rural house, such as the flat red-brick wall and 30-degree sloped roof. The new houses actually contributed to the loss of traditional architectural attributes and regional architectural cultures. The official architecture press published a series of manuals for constructing the new socialist village. Two in particular fostered the rigid copy-and-paste aesthetic that characterized new socialist village design all over vast rural China: «Manual for Master Plan of New Socialist Village» and «Manual for Building Design of New Socialist Village [...] The principal goal of the new socialist village is to offer a higher standard of living, creating an acceptable residential and infrastructural estate. In general, the contribution to this goal of planners, urban designers, and architects is banal and unreasonably homogenous master plans and architecture. In other words, building the new villages is considered a project of engineering and systems; function is privileged above all other aspects, including culture, crop-field context, and ecology»[17].

Despite the accidental - and in some cases critical - condition, the informal development of Zhagyang still had the potentiality of proposing more delicate and sensitive approaches without ultimately compromising the cultural inheritance. The cases of Jiankou and Zhangyang portray a tricky but potentially promising picture. One aspect appears clear and has to be remarked: their outputs raise the necessity of finding more balanced relationships between local actors and development agencies. In particular, the idea that fast changes correspond with rapid improvements has to be challenged[18].

Another factor to consider relates to Koolhaas' idea of the countryside as a source of identity, mentioned in the first chapter. As a millennial civilization's cradle, Chinese ruralities encompass the tangible and intangible elements of a distinctive cultural root, which find no closer definition than heritage. Far from being considered an asset for the local development, due to their physical and cultural fragility, the built forms inherited from the past risk disappear, and together with them also an important part of Chinese historical civilization. The problem of losing the site's distinctiveness goes in parallel with the struggle for finding convincing design proposals both at the urban and architectural scales. Therefore, this era of transition is generating important losses that express in several ways. The most apparent of them is the complete vanishing of cultural relicts and the excessive growth of the rural settlements due to villages' relocation and merging. On one side, many settlements, mainly along the coast, have grown to host more than 30.000 residents, assuming urban-like features. On the other side, a tremendous number of villages is vanishing, as reported in November 2017 during the 3rd China Ancient Villages and Towns Conference held in Beijing, when it has been pinpointed that between 2000 and 2010, the number of natural villages in China dropped sharply from 3,63 million to 2,71 million, with an average of 80 to 100 villages disappearing every day.

Top-down processes are consolidating farmlands while bottom-up ones erode them, ultimately compressing arable soil's quota. Many rural settlements consist of patchworks of residential compounds mixed with industrial and service districts, cookie-cutter neighborhoods, huge working sites, unfinished skeletons, abandoned ruins, disconnected infrastructural networks, and situations of «environmental instability» that generate a fragmentary and incoherent landscape. The common and most evident spatial feature is the loss of any difference between center and periphery, inducted by discontinuous growth and crisis cycles. Countryside's urbanization shows pervasive patterns where design disciplines struggle to find a compelling and acknowledged societal role. If in bottom-up spontaneous processes, this can be comprehended insofar economic possibilities are limited to the private initiative, in top-down planned transformations emerges a profound retreat of design place-making capacity, often resulting in utilitarian instruments manipulated by other forces. The urbanization or marginalization of villages, their prosperity or poverty, are just a few of the countless contradictions that pervade rural settlements during this transition time.

The Theoretical Framework of Rural Revitalization

The current political course has identified urbanizing and modernizing the countryside as the principal means to achieve a more harmonic rural-urban integration. The RR is the current and last step of the Chinese development policies dedicated to the countryside restructuring conceived by the political and cultural agendas. This chapter draws attention to its theoretical framework, tracing the conceptual origins and evolutionary paths to shed light on the new perspectives envisioned by its institutional dimension. In particular, we try to place the extent of RR against the backdrop of *Building a Moderately Prosperous Society* and *Ecological Civilization* notions, which encompass the Chinese visions of development for future generations.

A synthesis of the policies released by the central government was made by the China Development Research Foundation, remarking few significant shifts over the past decades. The Group identified three eras: in the 1980s, Chinese ruralities experienced «invigorating» policies; in the 1990s, «stabilizing» policies; and, since the 2000s, rural development has entered a new stage, with «repay the countryside» policies[1]. These politics share the point that, since the 1980s, the central government issued measures oriented towards a socialist market economy, which eventually blossomed out in state capitalism.

Over the last five-year development plans, the rural development occupied a core position within Central Document No. 1 and represented the principal argument for mitigating socioeconomic disparities between the urban and the rural. Its theoretical background, general principles, and implementation modes have evolved and assumed distinctive characters before consolidating in the notion of RR. The theoretical discourse and political narration have kept abreast in the last decades, generating fruitful intellectual alliances and embarrassing ambiguities to external eyes, mostly due to rhetoric emphasis.

The work by Wen Tiejun has been acknowledged to be the turning point that scientifically framed the rural issue. In 2003, when he was Professor at the School of Agriculture and Rural Development of the Renmin University of China and the main supporter of rural reconstruction in contemporary China, he stigmatized his well-known «Three Rural Issues». The three rural issues, which are village sustainability, agricultural security, and farmers' rights, became the benchmark to Beijing's Establishment and whoever wanted to deal with countryside restructuring. According to Wen, the ongoing agricultural modernization was not sufficient to mitigate the rural-urban gap. Wen stressed the necessity of exploring a more peasantry-focused and community-based rural development model. He found that the outflow of agricultural products from rural to urban areas, compromising the «property and income distribution system inherent in the small-scale peasant economy»[2], had generated inexperienced tensions and disparities. Another problem raised by Wen concerned the national development strategy, which endeavored «industrial capital, international trade, and economic globalization». Such a development model has overloaded farmers with duties bigger than their possibilities, putting China in a position vulnerable to «global shocks or financial crisis» because it relied on the market economy and importations. Wen was somehow reconciling the perplexities of Lester Brown on food security and self-reliance. More recently, during a conference held in Beijing in March 2017, Wen presented new problems affecting the countryside.

> First, and foremost, the trade surplus, which he sees impacting countryside production facilities. Another crisis is China's reliance on Western farming methods, which will have to change due to the resulting soil, water, and climate degradation. China will need to revert back to its 40 centuries of experience of regenerative farming and permaculture[3].

Wen's alarm cry stigmatized the problems and challenges of rural areas for the following political courses. The first effect was the release of the *Building a New Socialist Countryside* – BNSC – policy in 2006[4]. BNSC policy defined the core tasks, among which agricultural modernization, rural governance innovation, the expansion of social welfare, the strengthening of rural education, fiscal reform. Regarding urbanization, the policy stimulated local governments to formulate and implement their strategies for the on-field application of programs and evaluation of mechanisms. An essential aspect of BNSC was the relocation and concentration of natural villages into denser settlements, often the townships, in the form of «urban(ized) new rural neighborhoods»[5]. During this phase, the traditional patterns of rural society were seen as obstacles to national development, mainly due to the inappropriate use of natural resources and the runaway processes of land consumption. In response, the notion of "land consolidation" was devised by scholars to describe the practices targeted to optimize the use of land as

> a spatial problem-solving technique that attempts to eliminate certain types of land fragmentation and to improve land productivity through a process of concentration of plots, which is usually accompanied by the construction of new roads, irrigation facilities and other auxiliary services[6].

In regard to this, in 2012, China issued the National Land Consolidation Plan (2011–2015) to alleviate the food security problem, intending to realize high-quality, productive farmland for a total amount of 26.670.000 hectares. The plan stressed the necessity of building 300.000 hectares of housing surface in the countryside to rationalize rural settlements' layouts. Land consolidation was often carried out via land requisition and people relocation, causing social tensions sometimes[7].

Coming back to the BNSC policy, it was structured as a holistic policy to define a

> macro-economic development strategy aiming at rural restructuring under globalization, [where] a "new countryside" means advanced production, improved livelihood, clean and tidy villages, a civilized social atmosphere and efficient management[8].

These goals resonated as a direct answer to the three rural problems highlighted by Wen Tiejun. The «advanced production» was intended to be achieved by implementing modern agriculture using adequate techniques, structures, logistics, and complimentary services. The purpose of «clean and tidy villages» was targeted to improve villages' appearance and sustainability by encouraging the use of carbon-free fuels, improving the infrastructural network, such as roads, power, and running water, and elaborating village plans for demolitions and reconstructions. The policy suppressed the agricultural tax (2004) and, in parallel, the revenue increased gradually, securing farmers the possibility of improving livelihood means. Especially in the most impoverished areas, the policy enhanced agriculture's productivity and alleviated peasants' burdens. Significant efforts were put into education, abolishing the school fees up through grade 9 and providing free textbooks to needy students. It introduced a nationwide rural health insurance program as well as financial incentives to help peasants with production investments. BNSC policy was also an answer to the decaying rural society, apparently guided «neither by socialist norms nor by traditional morality» at the turn of the millennium[9]. The Ministry of Civil Affairs suggested that welfare services and appearance improvements had to be integrated into new compounds made by 1000 - 1500 dwellings. These new neighborhoods had to be arranged in blocks and defined by clear boundaries, even walled according to the developer preference, resonating ultimately, to my sensibility, as urban gated communities[10]. Despite the BNSC as a macro-policy was intended to concentrate on comprehensive rural development, some observers argued that it ignored the regional discrepancies in terms of geographical and economic conditions.

As noted by Pola, in 2007, the Urban Planning Law became the Urban and Rural Planning Law, inducing villages' administrations to study «a 20-year master plan for redevelopment»[11]. The notion of "urban-rural planning" entered the vocabulary of decision-makers and planners. Working with Provincial governments, they started proposing strategic regional development to mitigate the rural-urban disparities. The price for widespread prosperity was to burden on ecosystems, whose integrity went progressively under threat. In his book *The struggle for sustainability in Rural China*, Bryan Tilt declared that Chinese people could appear ecologically apathetic because of a supposed-to-be short-term vision that both weakened the care for pollution's risks and shaped the environmental consciousness negatively[12]. From one side, the expression «too poor to be green» made a point remarking that, in a country like China, facing a severe phase of transition, only a part of the rural citizens could afford the «luxury» of worrying about environmental protection. On the other side, Tilt's book also detected already in 2010 trends of change, acknowledging the materialization of a new collective awareness, which was progressively moving Chinese residents to realize the importance of living in a healthy environment.

The signals recognized by Tilt were just the first sparks of the emerging theory of EC, which today represents the main framework for territorial governance. However, even though the notion of EC has strongly been advocated by academic elites and has proliferated in the mainstream media[13], it may be obscure to observers oblivious of the Chinese political narrative. The realization of an EC is not just a slogan, but a goal written in the Constitution of the People Republic of China in 2018, declaring the political will to develop the national territory in a sustainable way. EC is currently appointed as «the most significant Chinese state-initiated imaginary of our global future»[14]. A key point of this long-term vision is to promote a «prosperous, harmonious, and beautiful» nation, which sounds like a consequence of the *Building a Moderately Prosperous Society* theory, as was observed[15].

The EC is the ideology addressed by the political leadership to foster sustainable development, environmental protection, and climate change mitigation[16]. Indeed it is acknowledged that EC moves from the detrimental effects generated by a political course mostly sensible to economic growth as the privileged means to achieve consensus and stability. The concept was formulated for the first time in the 1960s in the Soviet Union by the scientific community in order to alleviate the environmental impact caused by the rampant industrial modernization on the global stage. China discovered the term EC in 1997 from an article published in the party's principal theoretical magazine, the *Qiushi*. Since then, the Establishment has increasingly adopted the concept until the recent inscription in the constitution[17].

Nevertheless, Clivio[18] and Goron[19] remark an interesting ambiguity enshrined in the two-fold temporal dimension of Chinese EC. On the one hand, the EC situates in the fourth acknowledged stage of Chinese society, after material civilization, spiritual civilization, and political civilization[20]. On the other hand, the EC is imposed as both a goal to achieve and, simultaneously, as a condition already instituted, somehow ready to be exported.

In the EC concept, Chinese scholars have identified a more environmentally friendly approach to Marxism, labeled "Organic Marxism", to address a softer approach to development[21]. From one side, the reduction of growth objectives, made possible by the Chinese population's growing well-being, contributed to limit the harmful practices of territorial transformation. On the other side, experiments with ecovillages started being fostered throughout the country[22]. An interesting political mechanism in the Chinese governance chain was the relationships between the central and the local governments. Local governments' achievements were measured by observing both economic growth and environmental improvements, making the local authorities responsible for ecological troubles[23].

The spreading ecological sensitivity proved to converge the people consensus, encouraging the party delegates to adapt the government line narration. Since the 2000s, the leaders made larger and more extensive use of ecological slogans by conjugating eco-friendly attributes with declarations about the necessity of industrial growth. Even though China was one important signatory to Agenda 21 (1992), the concept of sustainable development was stressed by President Jiang Zemin only in 1997, during the 15th National Congress. He advocated the elaboration of a «strategy of sustainability», a long-term approach coupling the protection of environmental resources with economic growth. In 2002, President Jiang invigorated his ideas during the following National Congress by listing the realization of a "moderately prosperous society" - a concept inherited from Confucian thinking - as one of his core priorities. It has been observed that the ecological orientation assumed by the political Establishment has reinforced and enlarged the space for appreciation and reappropriation of traditional wisdom[24].

Later on, the inseparability of environmental sensibility and growth dynamics has become one of the favorite arguments of President Xi. Among the neologisms created for China's green ambitions, he used the slogan «clear waters and lush mountains are gold and silver», to stress the idea that the territorial resources have inestimable value[25]. The slogan was coined by Xi Jinping himself in 2005 when he was Zhejiang Party Secretary. Xi used such expression during many conferences, such for instance in the Speech at the United Nations Office in Geneva, to emphasize the necessity of a green turn.

Proceeding from the new starting point, we will promote green development to achieve better economic performance. I have said for many times that green mountains and clear water are as good as mountains of gold and silver. To protect the environment is to protect productivity, and to improve the environment is to boost productivity. This simple fact is increasingly recognized by people[26].

During his work in Fujian and Zhejiang, Xi put his ideas into practice to drive the cadres and the masses to work together and boost a new economic development path. In his theory, the natural elements like mountains, water, forests, fields, and lakes had a very close symbiotic relationship with human beings and constituted together an organic «community of life». According to him, «a good ecological environment [...] [was] the fairest public product; it [...] [was] the most inclusive benefit of the people», and, more in general, an unavoidable step towards the realization of the Chinese nation's great rejuvenation. Xi explained that «only the strictest rule of law [...] [could] provide a reliable guarantee for the construction of ecological civilization»[27].

Xi argued that the relationship between economic development and ecological protection had to be effectively integrated into the concept of green development concerning all aspects of society. In the same path as Hu Jintao's thinking on EC, Xi stressed the necessity of establishing EC pilot zones to accumulate successful experiences to drive sustainable development throughout the country.

China's endorsement of sustainability aligned to most

of the foreign political agendas yet following a distinctive path[28]. Beijing's policymakers have persistently proposed a concept of development conjugating the attributes of "sustainable and beautiful"[29]. During the 18th National Congress of the Communist Party of China held in November 2012, for the first time, *Beautiful China* was addressed as the challenging goal of EC construction. Alongside an extensive campaign, Chinese commitment to EC has resulted in the academic arena in a growing body of studies integrating ethic and aesthetic meanings, generating intellectual bridges with similar Western positions[30]. The main difference from Western counterparts is that China has not - yet - questioned the implementation of energy-consuming models of consumptions, industrial development, or economic growth, which remain still the main drivers for achieving poverty alleviation, political stability, and, in general, a "moderately prosperous society"[31]. This is quite far from the Western assumption, according to which caring about sustainability means reconsidering lifestyles or consolidated habits and, somehow, sacrificing some little comforts for a larger end. The notion of happy degrowth, strongly supported by intellectuals like Serge Latouche[32], represented one of the extreme antagonistic positions to the Chinese idea of blending industrial development and ecological protection via technocratic solutions.

In Chinese authorized narration, "ecological" and "beautiful" appeared to be interchangeable attributes, and the idea of beauty lost part of its subjective connotations to situate in a sphere of meanings that could

71

be easily recognized and understand. This new vocabulary is shaping the collective consciousness stressing an indissoluble correspondence between the attributes of healthy, beautiful, eco-friendly, and sustainable development. This alliance has roots in Chinese classical culture that provides a possible interpretative key where the concept of aesthetic quality deviates from the Western one.

> In Chinese, for example, terms such as «lovely» (mei or meili), «pretty» (piaoliang), or «good» (shan) tend to relate more to outer appearance, taste, and goodness than any sense of an innate or divine «beauty». As a result, any consideration of Chinese aesthetics requires an understanding of beauty that significantly differs from Western artistic ideals based on mimesis and on an identification with godhead. The Western ideal of an intrinsic divine beauty is foreign to Chinese aesthetic thought, and its conceptual absence may find parallels in the argument that has sometimes been made of a lack of an ubiquitous divine law in China (...) Chinese architecture - palaces, pagodas, and even common dwellings - an edifice is judged beautiful not only by its outward form or visual appearance, but even more by its cultural symbology. This symbology is often focused on the word as a duplication of cosmic patterns and was embodied in the names of buildings, as well as through numerology, ornamentation, ordering of spatial elements, and choice of design prototypes[33].

Chen noted that Chinese environmental aesthetics went along with the concept of beauty, inheriting that ancient aesthetic consciousness vehiculated by divination folklores and other geomantic practices. The most famous is *fengshui*, which «has also an environmental dimension and practical side when it comes to residential place selection and urban planning, [...] [and] stresses the importance of the sense of beauty, especially from the natural environment»[34]. The natural elements like mountains, rivers, and woods were essential to defining a beautiful landscape, which, being propitious for the family's present and future generations, was also sustainable. Beyond this form of ancient Chinese aesthetic consciousness, Chen advocated that also a contemporary sensibility toward environmental beauty was spreading, arguing that

> to develop a sense of environmental beauty means precisely that we start appreciating and therefore treating our environment as a home. This involves accepting our closeness and belonging to the environment, and how much our life depends on it[35].

On the same trajectory, as early as 2007, the Department of Environmental Protection's vice minister pushed the extent of environmental protection towards a cultural dimension using these words:

> Why is environmental protection considered a cultural issue? One of the core principles of traditional Chinese culture is that of harmony between humans and nature. Different philosophies all emphasize the political wisdom of a balanced environment. Whether it is the Confucian idea of humans and nature becoming one, the Taoist view of the Tao reflecting nature, or the Buddhist belief that all living things are equal, Chinese philosophy has helped our culture to survive for thousands of years. It can be a powerful weapon in preventing an environmental crisis and building a harmonious society[36].

The measures related to the *Beautiful China* campaign contributed to disseminating techniques oriented towards environmental safeguards. In the same year, 2012, the Ministry of Agriculture issued a call for the realization of Beautiful Villages, listing 1000 settlements as pilot projects covering different aspects of rural development[37]. This policy, which was proclaimed as the necessary new stage of social development to rethink the rural question, ended up with similar strengths and weaknesses to the previous ones, including the recurrent and controversial patterns of top-down implementations. One of the principal obstacles remained the funding application procedure, which was based on a rigid ministerial subdivision. According to the project's primary vocation and scope, rural settlements could apply for different financing programs, which were in constant update. The programs' nature corresponded with the government's ministerial department. Accordingly, the Beautiful Villages and Beautiful Leisure Villages lists were managed by the Ministry of Agriculture (MOA); the Historical and Culture Villages by the Ministry of Housing and Urban-Rural Development (MOHURD) and the National Cultural Heritage Administration (NCHA); Traditional Villages by MOHURD, NCHA, the Ministry of Culture (MOC), and Ministry of Finance (MOF); Ecological Villages and Eco-civilization Villages, by the Ministry of Ecology and Environment (MEE)[38]. Such strong segregation created the premises for the standardization of the development strategies, leaving little space for inclusive approaches to rural re-activation. In other words, actions of protection were relegated to historic towns, actions of industrial and technological strengthening concerned villages not listed or without recognized heritage elements, and actions of environmental protection regarded sites abundant with natural resources. The application process was based on a «points-based system in which funding is apportioned based on the number of points won»[39].

Although the Chinese new ecological sensitivity is still far from reaching full and coherent implementation, it represents one of the most ambitious political programs targeted to activate an inclusive development of the territory strongly committed to the safeguard of the resources of the planet. A tangible effect of current policies is the recent institution of new Departments dedicated to the protection and stewardship of natural resources, which have been established at the different levels of government, renovating the extent of domestic ecological policies[40].

> We have too much debt in the ecological environment. If we don't take this work tightly from now on, the price will be even greater in the future… People will see a fundamental improvement in the environment and the country will reach the targets set for building a Beautiful China by 2035.

With these words, Xi Jinping opened the 19th National Congress of China's Communist Party when the State Council released the *Strategic Plan for Rural Revitalization 2018-2022*. The objectives and the contents of this strategic plan endorsed agricultural development as an alternative economic growth engine in a long-term vision. Against the backdrop of Xi Jinping's guiding ideology labeled as *Socialism with Chinese Characteristics for a New Era*, RR could be framed as an updated strategy coherent to "build a moderately prosperous society". In principles, the document set the guidelines for comprehensive planning in the countryside, including several fields, like economy, politics, culture, society, ecology, and Party construction[41]. This strategy was addressed as a «historic task» essential to complete China's modernization. The strategy pointed out that by 2020 an institutional framework and policy system had to be established. In that time, both the poverty condition and rural productivity would have been substantially improved. By 2035, «decisive» progress would have been accomplished in agricultural innovation and public services supply. By 2050, China was intended to have efficient agriculture, beautiful countryside, and well-off farmers. Among the priorities listed by the campaign, we can find to strengthen sanitary infrastructures, reorganize settlement schemes, provide services to support entrepreneurial innovation, and rethink public spaces[42].

Either top-down massive reconstruction and bottom-up informal expansions are altering rural habitats. They both produce denser built environments that neglect traditional rural virtues, such as the historical connection with the ground, to express pseudo urban socio-cultural values, resulting in architectural forms relatively redundant and ludicrous. The observed processes expressed the problematic condition of design in rural construction, compelled to serve other economic impulses not interested in place-making.

Nevertheless, this era of transition shows two significant elements featuring Chinese ruralities: their status is generally ameliorating, since peasants' living conditions are substantially and structurally improving, and the momentum reached by RR open vast spaces to orient countryside development towards desirable milieu, as the new rural awareness mentioned in the first chapter proves. This phase, which can be put in continuity with the transformations begun in the late 1970s, is far from being concluded and is likely to envision the Chinese countryside as a challenging field of experimentation where to test new forms of human settlements.

RR's political discourse has produced to date a fertile ground for a global academic and cultural debate focused on rural futures that may find in Chinese efforts significant benchmarks. Xi's leadership has the merit of posing environmental, economic, and cultural issues on the same level. By aligning priorities and future visions, this political course is defining the conceptual framework – legitimated and acknowledged – necessary to a development systematically oriented in an ecological sense. This titanic mobilization puts China in a leading position in exploring countryside revitalization trajectories on the global stage.

The main migration flows are still rural-urban

oriented, but in China, as well as in different parts of the world, signals of returns to the countryside have been observed recently[43]. Despite the blossom out of these promising arguments, the question about «how fundamentally must the relationship between what we now call urban and rural be rethought»[44] remains open and challenges the way practitioners address design in our era.

Notes

Design in the rural: China as an observatory for research and design

1. B. Hillman & J. Unger, 'Editorial. The Urbanisation of Rural China', *China Perspective* vol. 3, 2013, p. 3.

2. Between 2015 and 2020 I was enrolled in the Ph.D. program *Architectural Urban Interior Design* hosted by the Department of Architecture and Urban Studies of Politecnico di Milano, supervisors Prof. Ilaria Valente and Prof. Luca Maria Francesco Fabris. From 2017 to 2020 I was enrolled in the Ph.D Program in *Design* of the School of Design of the Shanghai Jiao Tong University, supervisors Prof. Ma Wenjun and Prof. Huang Jianyun.

3. The proposal was curated the research group named «Sino-Italian Partnership Project in Urbanization for the Development programming for Zhangyang Village, Hanjiang, Putian» and was coordinated by Prof. Ma Wenjun. The delegation from Politecnico di Milano was composed by Prof. Ilaria Valente, Prof. Luca Maria Francesco Fabris, Ph.D. arch. Francesca Berni, and Ph.D. arch. Gerardo Semprebon.

4. R. Koolhaas, 'Ignored realm', in Amo / R. Koolhaas, *Countryside, a report*, Taschen, New York, pp. 2-3.

5. N. Cross, 'Designerly ways of knowing', *Design Studies,* vol. 3, no. 4, 1982, p. 221.

6. B. Rudofsky, *Architecture without architects*, MOMa Press Release, New York, 1964.

7. C. C. M. Lee, ed., *Taiqian. The Countryside as a City*, Harvard University Graduate School of Design, Cambridge MA, 2015, p. 4

8. A. Stokman, S. Ruff, 'Designing for an Urban Countryside', in B. de Meulder et al. eds., *Village in the City*, Park Books, Zurich, 2014; A. Stokman & S. Ruff, 'Beijing's New Urban Countryside – Designing with Complexity and Strategic Landscape Planning', *Journal of Landscape Architecture* vol. 3, no. 2, 2008, p. 30-45.

9. J. Bolchover & J. Lin, *Rural Urban Framework. Transforming the Chinese Countryside*, Birkhauser, Basel, 2014; C. Lange et al., *Homecoming. Contextualizing, Materializing and Practicing the Rural* *in China*, Gestalten, Berlin, 2013; P. Valle, *Rural Urban Framework*, Libria, Melfi, 2016.

10. J. Bolchover et al., 'Where is the Rural in an Urban World?' *Architectural Design* vol. 86, 2016, pp. 06-13.

11. P. Schumacher, 'Don't waste your time in the countryside?' *Architectural Design* vol. 86, 2016, pp. 128-133.

12. X. Zhang, ed., *Beautiful Villages. Rural Construction Practice in Contemporary China*, transl. He Yanfei, Images Publishing, Victoria, 2018.

13. X. Li, ed., *Building a Future Countryside*, Catalogue of the Chinese Pavilion at the 16th Biennale of Venice Architectural International Exhibition, The Images Publishing Group/ACC Art Books, New York, 2018.

14. W. Jun et al., *Rural Moves. The Songyang Story*, Aedes, Berlin, 2018.

15. H. Commerel, 'The New Rural Self-Confidence in China and the Global Challenge' in X. Li, *Building a Future Countryside*, Catalogue of the Chinese Pavilion at the 16th Biennale of Venice Architectural International Exhibition, The Images Publishing Group/ACC Art Books, New York, 2018, pp. 8-11.

16. N. Ou, *Utopia in Practice. Bishan Project and Rural Reconstruction*, Palgrave Macmillan, Singapore, 2020; N. Ou, *Bishan Commune: how to start your own Utopia*, OVO Press and Antipyrine, Copenhagen, 2015.

17. X. Tiantian, 'Rural, Reconsidered', TRANSFER Global Architecture Platform [website], July 2020. Accessed 14 Jan 2021.

18. R. Koolhaas Rem, op. cit., pp. 2-3.

19. Interview with Prof. Sun Zhe held in Beijing in November 2019 at the Beijing University of Civil Engineering and Architecture. The complete interview is also available in F. Seghezzi & K. R. Panta Bellido, 'Rural Edge. Project for a Research Center in Zhang Yang Village, Fujian Province, China'. Master Degree in Architecture Thesis, Supervisors M. Bovati, and G. Semprebon, Politecnico di Milano, 2020.

20. Bolchover et al., op. cit., pp. 06-13.

21. F. Jullien, *Living Off Landscape: Or, the Unthought-of in Reason*, transl. Rodriguez, Pedro, Rowman & Littlefield, London, 2018, p. 72.

22. J. B. Cobb & A. Vltchek, *China and Ecological Civilization*, Badak Merah Semesta, Jakarta, 2019, p. 54.

Migrant workers: a chance to rethink rural and urban status

1. X. Qiu, *A Loyal Character Dancer*, Sceptre, London NW1, 2002, p. 37.
2. F. Wu et al., eds., *Rural migrants in urban China. Enclaves and transient urbanism*, Routledge, London and New York, 2015.
3. China Development Research Foundation, *China's rural areas. Building a moderately prosperous society*, Routledge, London and New York, 2017, p. xvii.
4. M. K. Whyte, ed., *One Country, Two Societies: Rural-Urban Inequality in Contemporary China*, Harvard University Press, Cambridge, MA-London, 2010.
5. B. Tilt, *The struggle for sustainability in rural China*, Columbia University Press, New York, 2010, p. 12.
6. The ratio between urban and rural revenues reached its peak in 1994 when the income per capita of the former was 2.86 higher than their counterparts
7. M. K. Whyte, op. cit., p. 16; R. Zavoretti, *Rural Origins, City Lives: Class and Place in Contemporary China*, University of Washington Press, Seattle, 2016; R. Murphy, *How Migrant Labor is Changing Rural China*, Cambridge University Press, Cambridge, UK, 2002.
8. F. Wu et al., *Rural migrants in urban China*.
9. J. Bolchover & J. Lin, *Rural Urban Framework*, p. 128.
10. World Bank, *Urban China: Toward Efficient, Inclusive, and Sustainable Urbanization*, The World Bank, Washington DC, 2014, p. 10.
11. X. Ren, 'Socially engaged architecture in a Chinese rural village: Xihe Village Community Centre, 2014', *Architectural Research Quarterly*, vol. 20, no. 2, 2016, p. 120.
12. G. Marrucci, *Cemento rosso. Il secolo cinese, mattone dopo mattone*, Mimesis, Milano-Udine, 2017, p. 49.
13. World Bank, *Urban China*, op. cit., p. xvii. See also: S. Li, *Unemployment, inequality and poverty in urban China*, Routledge, London, 2012.
14. M. Meriggi, *L'architettura del continuo urbano-rurale in Cina. Insediamenti Hakka nel Guangdong Orientale*, Araba Fenice, Torino, 2018.
15. Y. Liu et al., 'The process and driving forces of rural hollowing in China under rapid urbanisation', *Journal of Geographical Sciences*

vol. 20 no. 6, 2010, pp. 876-888.
16. P. Ho et al., eds., *Rural Development in Transitional China*, Routledge, London, 2004.
17. From the "Strategic plan for Rural Revitalization (2018-2022)." The document's full-text is available at: https://www.jqknews.com/news/74365-The_State_Council_issued_the_strategic_plan_for_Rural_Revitalization_(2018-2022_years).html (English version), https://mp.weixin.qq.com/s/1HLIeOPfx7miDm77c0qL7Q (Chinese version). Last visit: October 18th, 2018.
18. L. R. Brown, *Who will feed China?*, Earthscan, London, 1995.

A Journey through Ordinary Practices of Rural Development

1. L. M.F. Fabris, & G. Semprebon, 'The chinese 'high and slender' condominium', *Techne – Journal of Technology for Architecture and Environment*, vol. 17, 2019, pp. 100-109.
2. C. C. M. Lee, ed., *Taiqian. The Countryside as a City*, op. cit., p. 13.
3. See: A. L. Ahlers, 'Weaving the Chinese Dream on the Ground? Local Government Approaches to "New-Typed" Rural Urbanization', *Journal of Chinese Political Science* vol. 20, 2015, pp. 121–142; C. Chen et al., 'Behavioral logics of local actors enrolled in the restructuring of rural China: A case study of Haoqiao Village in northern Jiangsu', *Journal of Rural Studies*, 2019, DOI: https://doi.org/10.1016/j.jrurstud.2019.01.021, article in press; Z. Zhang et al., 'Factors influencing rural households' willingness of centralized residence: Comparing pure and nonpure farming areas in China, *Habitat International* vol. 73, 2018, pp. 25-33; W. Liu et al., 'Impacts of concentrated rural resettlement policy on rural restructuring in upland areas: A case study of Qiantang Town in Chongqing, China', *Land Use Policy* vol. 77, 2018, pp. 732-744; L. Shen et al., 'Why small towns can not share the benefits of urbanization in China?', *Journal of Cleaner Production* vol. 174, 2018, pp. 728- 738.
4. G. E. Guldin, *What's a Peasant to Do? A village becoming town in southern China*, Westview Press, Oxford, 2001, p. 7.
5. J. Bolchover & J. Lin, *Rural Urban Framework*, op. cit., p. 123.
6. Informal settlements have been developed in urban area too, in the so-called *urban villages*, which are former rural agglomerations inglobated by the expansion of mega-cities, especially in coastal regions. See: S. Al, ed., *Villages in the City. A Guide to South China's*

Informal Settlements, Hong Kong University Press, Hong Kong, 2014.
7. R. G. Knapp, ed., *Chinese Landscapes: The Village as Place*, University of Hawaii's Press, Honolulu, 1992, p. 66.
8. Y. Yan, 'Making room for intimacy. Domestic space and conjugal privacy in rural North China', in R. G. Knapp & K. Lo, eds., *House, home, family. Living and Being Chinese*, University of Hawai'i Press, Beijing, 2005, p. 373-396.
9. R. G. Knapp, & K. Lo, eds., *House, home, family. Living and Being Chinese*, University of Hawaii's Press, Honolulu, 2005, p. 225.
10. Y. Yan, 'Making room for intimacy., op. cit., p. 373-396.
11. The research group mentioned above.
12. "Xi Jinping's green development concept: perfecting the 'top design' and strengthening the four beams and eight columns," People's Network 2017-06-06. Retrieved from http://jyds.ncvt.cn/ljsmjcmx/en/rmfzsiji.php?id=92&ipage=2. Last visit October 2018 21st.
13. G. Semprebon Gerardo et al., 'Earthen buildings in rural Fujian. Architectural challenges for local development,' in S. Yong et al., ed., *Vernacular and earthern architecture towards local development.* Tongji University Press, Shanghai, pp. 358-365.
14. G. Semprebon et al., 'Vernacular architecture as a form of resilience in Chinese countryside transition. Evidence from a rural settlement in the Fujian province', *Int. ISPRS - International Archives of the Photogrammetry, Remote Sensing and Spatial Information Sciences*, vol. XLIV-M-1-2020, pp. 181–188.
15. G. Semprebon Gerardo et al., 'Shaping a future countryside. Light and shadow on townships settlement's model in Chinese urban-rural continuum', *Środowisko Mieszkaniowe – Housing Environment*, vol. 23, 2019, pp. 45-51.
16. J. Wang & X. Wang, 'Transition of Chinese urban-rural planning at the new-type urbanization stage', *Frontiers of Architectural Research* vol. 4, no. 4, 2015, pp. 341-343; Y. Chu, 'China's new urbanization plan: Progress and structural constraints', *Cities* vol. 103, 2020, pp. 1-10.
17. C. C. M. Lee, *Taiqian. The Countryside as a City*, op. cit., p. 33.
18. G. Semprebon et al., 'Towards Design Strategies for Requalifying the Rural: A Comparative Study of Hollow Settlements in China and Italy', *KnE Social Sciences* vol. 3 no. 27, 2019, pp. 195–208.

The Theoretical Framework of Rural Revitalization

1. China Development Research Foundation, *China's rural areas,*op. Cit., p. 336.

2. See: T. Wen, 'Deconstructing modernization', *Chinese Sociology and Anthropology*, vol. 39, no. 4, 2007, pp. 10-25; J. Pan et al., 'Three "centuries": the context and development of rural construction in China', *Inter-Asia Cultural Studies*, vol. 18, no. 1, 2017, pp. 120-130.

3. See: T. Wen, *Sannong wenti yu shiji fansi* [The Three Rural Problems and Some Reflections at the End of the Twentieth Century], Joint Publishing, Beijing 2005, quoted in N. Ou, 'Social Change and Rediscovering Rural Reconstruction in China', in S. Jeong & T. Morris-Suzuki, eds., *New Worlds from Below. Informal life politics and grassroots action in twenty-first-century Northeast Asia*, ANU Press, Acton, 2017.

4. A. L. Ahlelrs, *Rural policies implementation in contemporary China*, Routledge, London, 2014, p. 3.

5. Ibid., p. 71.

6. H. Long et al., 'Building new countryside in China: A geographical perspective', *Land Use Policy* vol. 27, 2010, pp. 457-470.

7. Z. Qian, 'Resettlement and adaptation in China's small town urbanization: Evidence from the villagers' perspective', *Habitat International* vol. 67, 2017, pp. 33-43.

8. A. L. Ahlers & G. Schubert, '"Building a New Socialist Countryside" – Only a Political Slogan?', *Journal of Current Chinese Affairs*, vol. 38, no. 4, 2009, pp. 35-62.

9. S. Thøgersen, 'Revisiting a Dramatic Triangle: The State, Villagers, and Social Activists in Chinese Rural Reconstruction Projects', *Affairs* vol. 4, 2009, pp. 9-33.

10. L. Rosenberg, 'Urbanising the Rural. Local strategies for creating "new style" rural communities in China', *China Perspectives* vol. 3, 2013, pp. 63-71.

11. A. Pola, 'Reframing Chinese Villages', *Modu Magazine*, 2019. Available at: https://www.modumag.com/focus/reframing-chinese-villages/#_ftn1 (last access on November 2019, the 25th).

12. B. Tilt, *The struggle for sustainability in rural China*, op. cit.

13. J. Heurtebise, 'Sustainability and Ecological Civilization in the Age of Anthropocene: An Epistemological Analysis of the Psychosocial and 'Culturalist' Interpretations of Global Environmental Risks',

Sustainability vol. 9, 2017, p. 1331.

14. M. H. Halskov et al., 'Ecological civilization: Interpreting the Chinese past, projecting the global future', *Global Environmental Change* vol. 53, 2018, pp. 195-203.

15. China Development Research Foundation, *China's rural areas*, op. cit.

16. F. Spagnoli, 'La riforma della Costituzione cinese: un'analisi della revisione costituzionale del 2018 e dei suoi caratteri principali', *DPCE Online* vol. 38, no. 1, 2019, pp. 129-163.

17. O. Krischer & L. Tomba, eds., *Shades of Green: Notes on China's Eco-civilisation*, Made in China, Sidney, 2020.

18. C. Clivio, 'La civiltà ecologica della nuova era di Xi Jinping', *Sinosfere*, vol. 7, 2019. Available at: http://sinosfere. com/2019/10/01/carlotta-clivio-la-civilta-ecologica-della-nuova-era-di-xi-jinping/. Last access on September 2020, the 3rd.

19. C. Goron, 'Ecological Civilisation and the Political Limits of a Chinese Concept of Sustainability', *China Perspectives* vol. 4, 2018, pp. 39-52.

20. A. Gare, *The Philosophical Foundations of Ecological Civilization: A manifesto for the future*, Routledge, New York, 2017; S. Geall & A. Ely, 'Narratives and pathways towards an ecological civilisation in contemporary China', *China Quarterly*, vol. 236, 2018, pp. 1175-1196.

21. P. Clayton & A. W. M. Schwartz, *What is ecological civilization? Crisis, Hope, and the Future of the Planet*, Process Century Press, Anoka, MN, 2019, p. 84.

22. J. B. Cobb & A. Vltchek, *China and Ecological Civilization*, op. cit., p. 9.

23. Ibid., p. 45.

24. Ibid., p. 56.

25. M. H. Halskov et al., 'Ecological civilization', op. cit., pp. 195-203.

26. S. Meng, 'An Insight into the Green Vocabulary of the Chinese Communist Party', *Chinadialogue*, vol. 15 November 2012, https://www.chinadialogue.net/article/show/single/en/5339-An-insight-into-the-green-vocabulary-of-the-Chinesecommunist-party.

27. J. Xi, 'Work Together to Build a Community of Shared Future for Mankind', Speech at the United Nations Office in Geneva, CGTN, 18th January 2017, https://america.cgtn.com/2017/01/18/full-text-of-xi-jinping-keynote-speechat-the-united-nations-office-in-geneva. Last visit October 2018, the 20th.

28. D. Brombal & A. Moriggi, 'Institutional Change in China's Sustainable Urban Development', *China Perspectives* vol. 1, 2017, pp. 45-56; F. Jullien, *Living Off Landscape,* op. cit.

29. M. Marinelli, 'How to Build a 'Beautiful China' in the Anthropocene. The Political Discourse and the Intellectual Debate on Ecological Civilization', *Journal of Chinese Political Science*, vol. 23, 2018, pp. 365–386.

30. E. Turri, *Il paesaggio come teatro. Dal territorio vissuto al territorio rappresentato*, Marsilio, Venezia, 1998; M. Venturi Ferriolo, *Etiche del paesaggio. Il progetto del mondo umano*, Ed. Riuniti, Roma, 2002.

31. A. Curtis et al., eds., *Sustainable development in China*, Routledge, London-New York, 2013.

32. D. H. Meadows et al., *The Limits to Growth: The 30-year Update*, Chelsea Green Publishing, White River Junction, Vermont, 2004.

33. S. Bush & S. Hsiao-yen, *Early Chinese Texts on Painting*, Harvard University Press, Cambridge, MA, 1985, p. 2.

34. W. Chen, *Chinese Environmental Aesthetics*, Su Feng (transl.), Cipriani, Gerald (ed.), Routledge, London, 2015, p. 11.

35. Ibid., p. 180.

36. See: J. Xi, '"Green Water Qingshan is Jinshan Yinshan". Delineating the Ecological Red Line Promoting Green Development', *People's Network - China Communist Party News Network* 05th June 2017, retrieved from: http://jyds.ncvt.cn/ljsmjcmx/en/rmfzsiji. php?id=94&ipage=3. Last visit in October 2018 21st.

37. X. Zhang, ed., *Beautiful Villages.* Op. cit., p. 14.

38. A. Pola, 'When Heritage Is Rural: Environmental Conservation, Cultural Interpretation and Rural Renaissance in Chinese Listed Villages', *Built Heritage* vol. 2, 2019, pp. 64-80.

39. T. Lincoln & R. Madgin, 'The inherent malleability of heritage: creating China's beautiful villages', *International Journal of Heritage Studies*, vol. 9, no. 24, 2018, pp. 938-953.

40. Conversation with Prof. Ma Wenjun (Shanghai Jiao Tong University) occurred on November 2019, the 16th in Beijing, during the IV Beijing International Urban Design Forum, held at Beijing University of Civil Engineering and Architecture.

41. V.A., 'China's Rural Vitalization Strategy', *China Pictorial,* vol. 836, 2018, p. 16-41; see also: *Strategic plan for Rural Revitalization (2018-2022)*. The document's full-text is available at: https://www. jqknews.com/news/74365-The_State_Council_issued_the_strategic_ plan_for_Rural_Revitalization_(2018-2022_years).html (English version), https://mp.weixin.qq.com/s/1HLIeOPfx7miDm77c0qL7Q (Chinese version). Last visit: October 31th, 2020.

42. H. Long, *Land Use Transitions and Rural Restructuring in China*, Springer, Singapore, 2020; Y. Liu et al., 'China's rural revitalization and development: Theory, technology and management', *Journal of Geographical Sciences*, vol. 30, ,o. 12, 2020, pp. 1923–1942.

43. J. B. Cobb, *China and Ecological Civilization*, op. cit., p. 16.

44. P. Clayton & A. W. M. Schwartz, *What is ecological civilization?* Op. cit., p. 103.

Bibliography

- Ahlers, A. L., *Rural policy implementation in contemporary China,* Routledge, London, 2014.
- Ahlers, A. L., 'Weaving the Chinese Dream on the Ground? Local Government Approaches to "New-Typed" Rural Urbanization', *Chinese journal of political science,* vol. 20, no. 2, 2015, pp. 121-142.
- Ahlers, A. L. & G. Schubert, '"Building a New Socialist Countryside" – Only a Political Slogan?', *Journal of Current Chinese Affairs,* vol. 38, no. 4, 2009, pp. 35-62.
- Ai, S., *Villages in the City. A Guide to South China's Informal Settlements,* Hong Kong University Press, Hong Kong, 2014.
- Bolchover, J. et al., 'Where is the Rural in an Urban World?', *Architectural Design,* vol. 86, 2016, pp. 6-13.
- Bolchover, J. & J. Lin, *Rural urban framework. Transforming the Chinese countryside,* Birkhäuser, Basel, 2014.
- Brombal, D. & A. Moriggi, 'Institutional Change in China's Sustainable Urban Development: A Case Study on Urban Renewal and Water Environmental Management', *China Perspectives,* vol. 1, 2017, pp. 45-56.
- Brown, L. R., *Who will feed China?,* Earthscan, London, 1995.
- Bush, S. & H. Shih, *Early Chinese Texts on Painting,* Harvard University Press, Cambridge, Massachussets, 1985.
- Chen, C. et al., 'Behavioral logics of local actors enrolled in the restructuring of rural China: A case study of Haoqiao Village in northern Jiangsu', *Journal of Rural Studies,* 2019, in press.
- Chen, W., *Chinese Environmental Aesthetics,* Routledge, London, 2015.
- China Development Research Foundation, *China's rural areas. Building a moderately prosperous society,* Routledge, London and New York, 2017.
- Chu, Y., 'China's new urbanization plan: Progress and structural constraints', *Cities,* vol. 103, 2020, pp. 1-10.

- Clayton, P. & A. Schwartz, *What Is Ecological Civilization? Crisis, Hope, and the Future of the Planet,* Process Century Press, Anoka, 2019.
- Clivio, C., 'La civiltà ecologica della nuova era di Xi Jinping', *Sinosfere,* vol. 7, 2019.
- Cobb, J. B. & A. Vltchek, *China and Ecological Civilization,* Badak Merah Semesta, Jakarta, 2019.
- Commerel, H., 'The New Rural Self-Confidence in China and the Global Challenge' in Li, X. ed., *Building a Future Countryside,* The Images Publishing Group/ACC Art Books, New York, 2018, pp. 8-11.
- Cross, N., 'Designerly ways of knowing', *Design Studies,* vol. 3, no. 4, 1982, pp. 221-227.
- Curtis, A. et al., *Sustainable Development in China,* Routledge Ltd, London, 2013.
- Fabris, L.M.F., Semprebon G., 'The Chinese 'high and slender' condominium', *Techne - Journal of Technology for Architecture and Environment,* vol. 17, 2019, pp. 104-113.
- Gare, A., *The Philosophical Foundations of Ecological Civilization. A manifesto for the future,* Routledge, New York, 2017.
- Geall, S., Ely, A., 'Narratives and pathways towards an ecological civilisation in contemporary China', *China Quarterly*, vol. 236, 2018, pp. 1175-1196.
- Goron, C., 'Ecological Civilisation and the Political Limits of a Chinese Concept of Sustainability', *China Perspective,* vol. 4, 2018, pp. 39-52.
- Guldin, G. E., *What's a peasant to do?* Westview Press, Oxford, 2001.
- Hansen, M. H. et al., 'Ecological civilization: Interpreting the Chinese past, projecting the global future', *Global environmental change,* vol. 53, 2018, pp. 195-203.
- Heurtebise, J., 'Sustainability and Ecological Civilization in the Age of Anthropocene: An Epistemological Analysis of the Psychosocial and "Culturalist" Interpretations of Global Environmental Risks', *Sustainability,* vol. 9, no. 8, 2017, pp. 1331.
- Hillman, B. & J. Unger, 'Editorial. The Urbanisation of Rural China', *China Perspective,* vol. 3, 2013, pp. 3.

- Ho, P. et al., *Rural Development in Transitional China,* Routledge, London, 2004.
- Jullien, F., *Living Off Landscape,* Rowman & Littlefield International, London, 2018.
- Jun, W. et al., *Rural moves. The Songyang Story,* Aedes, Berlin, 2018.
- Knapp, R. G., *Chinese landscapes. The village as place,* University of Hawaii Press, United States, 1992.
- Knapp, R. G. & K. Lo, *House, home, family. Living and being Chinese.* University of Hawai'i Press, Beijing, 2005.
- Koolhaas, R., 'Ignored realm' in AMO and Rem Koolhaas ed., *Countryside, a report,* Taschen, New York, 2020, pp. 2-3.
- Krischer, O. & Tomba L., eds., *Shades of Green: Notes on China's Eco-civilisation*, Made in China, Sidney, 2020.
- Lange, C. et al., *Homecoming. Contextualizing, Materializing, and Practicing the Rural in China,* Gestalten, Berlin, 2013.
- Lee, C. C. M., *Taiqian. The Countryside as a City,* Harvard University Graduate School of Design, Cambridge, MA, 2015.
- Li, X., *Building a Future Countryside. Catalogue of the Chinese Pavilion at the 16th Biennale of Venice Architectural International Exhibition,* The Image Publishing Group / ACC Art Books, New York, 2018.
- Lincoln, T. & R. Madgin, 'The inherent malleability of heritage: creating China's beautiful villages', *International Journal of Heritage Studies,* vol. 24, no. 9, 2018, pp. 938-953.
- Liu, W. et al., 'Impacts of concentrated rural resettlement policy on rural restructuring in upland areas: A case study of Qiantang Town in Chongqing, China', *Land Use Policy,* vol. 77, 2018, pp. 732-744.
- Liu, Y. et al., 'The process and driving forces of rural hollowing in China under rapid urbanization', *Journal of Geographical Sciences,* vol. 20, no. 6, 2010, pp. 876-888.
- Liu, Y. et al., 'China's rural revitalization and development: Theory, technology and management', *Journal of Geographical Sciences,* vol. 30, no. 12, 2020, pp. 1923–1942.
- Long, H. et al., 'Building new countryside in China: A geographical perspective', *Land Use Policy,* vol. 27, no. 2, 2010, pp. 457-470.
- Marinelli, M., 'How to Build a 'Beautiful China' in the

Anthropocene. The Political Discourse and the Intellectual Debate on Ecological Civilization', *Chinese journal of political science,* vol. 23, no. 3, 2018, pp. 365-386.

- Marrucci, G., *Cemento rosso. Il secolo cinese, mattone dopo mattone,* Mimesis, Milano-Udine, 2017.
- Meadows, D. et al., *The Limits to Growth: The 30-year Update,* Chelsea Green Publishing, White River Junction, Vermont, 2004.
- Meng, S., 'An Insight into the Green Vocabulary of the Chinese Communist Party', *Chinadialogue,* vol. 15, 2012.
- Meriggi, M., *L'architettura del continuo urbano-rurale in Cina: insediamenti Hakka nel Guangdong orientale,* Araba Fenice, Torino, 2018.
- Meulder, B. d. et al., *Village in the city,* Park Books, Zürich, 2014.
- Murphy, R., *How Migrant Labor is Changing Rural China,* Cambridge University Press, Cambridge, UK, 2002.
- Ou, N., *Utopia in Practice: Bishan Project and Rural Reconstruction,* Palgrave Macmillan, Singapore, 2020.
- Ou, N., 'Social Change and Rediscovering Rural Reconstruction in China' in Jeong, S. E. and Tessa Morris-Suzuki ed., *New Worlds from Below. Informal life politics and grassroots action in twenty-first-century Northeast Asia,* ANU Press, Acton, 2017.
- Ou, N., *Bishan Commune: how to start your own Utopia,* OVO Press and Antipyrine, Copenhagen, 2015.
- Pan, J. et al., 'Three "centuries": the context and development of rural construction in China', *Inter-Asia Cultural Studies,* vol. 18, no. 1, 2017, pp. 120-130.
- Pola, A., 'Reframing Chinese Villages' [https://www.modumag.com/focus/reframing-chinese-villages/#_ftn1]2019a
- Pola, A., 'When Heritage Is Rural: Environmental Conservation, Cultural Interpretation and Rural Renaissance in Chinese Listed Villages.', *Built Heritage,* vol. 2, 2019b, pp. 64-80.
- Qian, Z., 'Resettlement and adaptation in China's small town urbanization: Evidence from the villagers' perspective', *Habitat International,* vol. 67, 2017, pp. 33-43.
- Qiu, X., *A Loyal Character Dancer,* Soho Press, New York, 2002.
- Ren, X., 'Socially engaged architecture in a Chinese rural village: Xihe Village Community Centre, 2014', *Architectural Research*

Quarterly, vol. 20, no. 2, 2016, pp. 119-130.

- Rosenberg, L., 'Urbanising the rural: local strategies for creating "new style" rural communities in China', *China Perspectives,* vol. 3, 2013, pp. 63-71.
- Rudofsky, B., *Architecture without architects,* MOMA Press Release, New York, 1964.
- Schumacher, P., 'Don't Waste Your Time in the Countryside', *Architectural design,* vol. 86, no. 4, 2016, pp. 128-133.
- Seghezzi, F. & Panta Bellido, K. R. 'Rural Edge. Project for a Research Center in Zhang Yang Village, Fujian Province, China'. Master Degree in Architecture Thesis, Supervisors M. Bovati, and G. Semprebon, Politecnico di Milano, 2020.
- Semprebon, G. et al., ' Vernacular architecture as a form of resilience in Chinese countryside transition. Evidence from a rural settlement in Fujian Province. ', *ISPRS - International Archives of the Photogrammetry, Remote Sensing and Spatial Information Sciences,* vol. XLIV-M-1-2020, 2020, pp. 181-188.
- Semprebon, G., Fabris, L.M.F., 'Shaping a future countryside. Light and shadow on rural settlement's models in Chinese urban-rural continuum', *rodowisko Mieszkaniowe,* vol. 26, 2019, pp. 45-51.
- Semprebon, G. et al., 'Earthen buildings in rural Fujian. Architectural challenges for local development' in Shao, Y. et al. ed., *Proceedings of the ICOMOS CIAV & ISCEAH 2019 China Joint Annual Meeting & International Conference on Vernacular & Earthen Architecture towards Local Development,* Tongji University Press, Shanghai, 2019, pp. 358-365.
- Semprebon, G. et al., 'Towards Design Strategies for Requalifying the Rural: A Comparative Study of Hollow Settlements in China and Italy', *2019 XJTLU International Conference: Architecture across Boundaries, KnE Social Sciences,* vol. 1, 2019, pp. 195-208.
- Shen, L. et al., 'Why small towns can not share the benefits of urbanization in China?', *Journal of Cleaner Production,* vol. 174, 2018, pp. 728-738.
- Shi, L., *Unemployment, inequality and poverty in urban China,* Routledge, London, 2012.
- Spagnoli, F., 'La riforma della Costituzione cinese: un'analisi

della revisione costituzionale del 2018 e dei suoi caratteri principali', *DPCE Online,* vol. 1, 2019, pp. 129-163.

- Stokman, A. et al., 'Designing for an Urban Countryside' in de Meulder, B. et al. ed., *Village in the city,* Park Books, Zurich, 2014.
- Stokman, A. et al., 'Beijing's New Urban Countryside – Designing with Complexity and Strategic Landscape Planning', *Journal of Landscape Architecture,* vol. 3, no. 2, 2008, pp. 30-45.
- Tiantian, X. 'Rural, Reconsidered', TRANSFER Global Architecture Platform [website], July 2020. Accessed 14 Jan 2021.
- Thøgersen, S., 'Revisiting a Dramatic Triangle: The State, Villagers, and Social Activists in Chinese Rural Reconstruction Projects', *Journal of Current Chinese Affairs,* vol. 38, no. 4, 2009, pp. 9-33.
- Tiejun, W., 'Deconstructing Modernization', *Chinese Sociology & Anthropology,* vol. 39, no. 4, 2007, pp. 10-25.
- Tiejun, W., 'Centenary reflections on the "three dimensional problem" of rural China', *Inter-Asia Cultural Studies,* vol. 2, no. 2, 2001, pp. 287-295.
- Tilt, B., *The struggle for sustainability in rural China,* Columbia University Press, New York, 2010.
- Turri, E., *Il paesaggio come teatro,* Marsilio, Venezia, 1998.
- V.A., 'China's Rural Vitalization Strategy', *China Pictorial,* vol. 836, 2018, pp. 16-41.
- Valle, P., *Rural urban framework,* Libria, Melfi, 2016.
- Venturi Ferriolo, M., *Etiche del paesaggio. Il progetto del mondo umano,* Editori Riuniti, Roma, 2002.
- Wang, J. & X. Wang, 'Transition of Chinese urban-rural planning at the new-type urbanization stage', *Frontiers of Architectural Research,* vol. 4, no. 4, 2015, pp. 341-343.
- Whyte, M. K., *One Country, Two Societies. Rural-Urban Inequality in Contemporary China,* Harvard University Press, Cambridge, MA, 2010.
- World Bank, *Urban China: Toward Efficient, Inclusive, and Sustainable Urbanization,* The World Bank, Washington, DC, 2014.
- Wu, F. et al., *Rural Migrants in Urban China. Enclaves and transient urbanism,* Routledge, London, 2013.

- Xiaochun, Z., *Beautiful villages. Rural construction practice in contemporary China*, Images Publishing, Victoria, 2018.
- Zavoretti, R., *Rural Origins, City Lives: Class and Place in Contemporary China,* University of Washington Press, Seattle, 2016.
- Zhang, Z. et al., 'Factors influencing rural households' willingness of centralized residence: Comparing pure and nonpure farming areas in China', *Habitat International,* vol. 73, 2018, pp. 25-33.

Village panorama. Conflictual relationship between a fragile historic building and a free-standing villa. Zhangyang Village, Fujian Province, 2018.

New rural settlement street view. Arrays of row houses replicated uniformly on the land. Jiankou Village, Fujian Province, 2017.

New rural settlement satellite view. Jiankou Village, Fujian Province. Author's ri-elaboration of a satellite image taken from Google Earth.

Auid Series: